Meeting the Needs of Disaffected Students

Meeting the Needs of Disaffected Students

Engaging students with social, emotional and behavioural difficulties

Dave Vizard

network
continuum

Continuum International Publishing Group
Network Continuum
The Tower Building   80 Maiden Lane, Suite 704
11 York Road   New York, NY 10038
London, SE1 7NX

www.networkcontinuum.co.uk
www.continuumbooks.com

British Library Cataloguing-in-Publication Data
A catalogue record for this book is available from the British Library.

ISBN: 9780826434654 (paperback)

Library of Congress Cataloguing-in-Publication Data
Vizard, Dave.
  Meeting the needs of disaffected students: engaging students with
social, emotional, and behavioural difficulties/Dave Vizard.
        p. cm.
  Includes bibliographical references and index.
  ISBN 978-0-8264-3465-4 (pbk. : alk. paper) 1. Children with social
disabilities–Education–Great Britain. 2. Motivation in
education–Great Britain. 3. Problem youth–Behavior
modification–Great Britain. I. Title.
  LC4096.G7V59 2009
  371.93–dc22

2009009022

Typeset by YHT Ltd, London
Printed and bound in Great Britain by the MPG Books Group

Contents

Acknowledgements

This book is dedicated to the memory of my mum, Ruth, who always gave me so much support and inspiration. Also to the memory of my sister-in-law, Elizabeth, a great storyteller, who always saw the positive side of life and is greatly missed. Thanks to my family, Annwyn, Emma and Tim for all their support and in particular to my wife Annwyn who gave me so much encouragement and help in producing this book and without whose support none of this would have been possible.

Special thanks and gratitude to all the students and staff I have worked with over many years in schools and colleges.

Introduction

Many students in schools are disaffected and find it difficult to connect with the learning process. They have low self-esteem and are often unable to manage their anger. The breakdown of the family unit, disorderly homes and inappropriate parenting has led to students arriving at school confused emotionally. Some students have turned to youth communities and gangs for support and role models. Mental health issues occur amongst many students with suicides, eating disorders and self-harm prevalent.

This book has been structured to enable teachers and support staff to re-engage disaffected students and ensure they have a successful learning experience and to show how we can best support them through a variety of approaches and techniques. It looks at developing emotional literacy, Neuro-Linguistic Programming and reviews a range of syndromes and conditions offering support strategies that will encourage the engagement of such students. It also looks at how we can develop approaches for students to self-manage their behaviour and how we can captivate their curiosity by making lessons fun by using a range of starter activities and brain breaks. It gives a model of how we can develop a consistent approach to managing disaffected students.

Each chapter includes a 'key points to remember' summary at the end. There are case studies in each chapter and lots of practical information on how to support disaffected students. Many strategies are set out in easy-to-read bullet lists. The book is loaded with practical ideas for engaging students.

1 Causes of disaffection

Many students arrive at school in a 'disrupted' state due to the confusing world in which they are growing up. It is little wonder that they become disaffected and disengaged from their learning. Professor Aynsley-Green (2007), the children's commissioner for England, stated: 'We are turning out a generation of young people who are unhappy, unhealthy, engaging in risky behaviour, who have poor relationships with their family and their peers, who have low expectations and don't feel safe.'

Low self-esteem as a result of the 'factory farming' approach to schooling has led to many learners feeling vulnerable as they have been tested regularly and in some cases this leads to reinforcing failure as they frequently gain poor results. Many students have developed work avoidance strategies and have found kudos by failing – they are good at being bad. The constraints of the National Curriculum, the testing culture and the inspectorial nature of schooling have led to a narrowing of the curriculum and a safety-first/risk-aversive approach by staff. Many learners have a perceived lack of ability and doubt the relevance of the curriculum. They are also receiving mixed messages about the various curricular pathways.

The 14–16 Increased Flexibility programme and the 14–19 Specialized Diplomas are now offering greater relevance to students and the experiences of schools working closely with colleges of further education have been good. The recent changes to assessment in Key Stage 3 and the removal of Standard Assessment Tests (SATs) at this stage have been helpful.

The breakdown of the family unit has led to a number of difficulties for students. Melanie Philips (2008) suggested young people are more aggressive due to disorderly homes. 'Catastrophic breakdown of parenting, emotional chaos and absence of love and care in their disorderly homes increasingly results in aggression as their instinctive response to the slightest setback.' Students do not have appropriate adult role models to support them. The disintegration of nuclear and extended families has led to formerly effective support mechanisms disappearing. In some cases overly complicated extended families have developed due to multiple relationships, which lead to contradictory messages being given. In many children's lives there is a total lack of appropriate role models. Patricia Morgan (2008) says that: 'Broken families and serial fathers produce homes full of conflict and chaos and they are terrible for children.' The Tellus 3 Survey of 150,000 10 to 15 year olds published by Ofsted (2008) report that fewer children say they have adults they can turn to with problems, which raises fears of a breakdown in communication between generations. The Prince's Trust, in its report on the Culture of Youth Communities (2008) said that young people were turning to youth communities/gangs for support rather than their parents as role models. In fact gangs and groups offer safety, a sense of identity and belonging and help raise self-esteem in many areas of extreme deprivation. In many of these gangs, drugs and violence have replaced the family.

Many parents feel helpless and give in to the 'pester power' of their children. A failure to set the firm boundaries that are required can cause problems. Parents themselves may not have experienced appropriate parenting and do not have the necessary skills. There appears to be a lack of affection and appropriate nurture. The Office for National Statistics (ONS), in a report funded by the Department for Health (2008) outlined the factors that protect and help students recover from emotional and behavioural problems. 'Social capital' factors such as networks of family and friends, clubs, groups and neighbourhood safety were linked to well-being. Some students have tremendous burdens placed on them and act as young carers to siblings and other family members.

Appendix A gives more details about the findings of the ONS Report, the Prince's Trust Report, the Good Childhood Inquiry and the Tellus 3 Survey.

Many young people are looked-after children and may in some cases have been placed with a number of alternative caretakers (for example, a number of foster carers). This can have an impact on these young people. Once they establish a good relationship with the carers they are often moved to a new location and so they learn to avoid making good relationships with adults because they believe they will be moved on. This is a significant contributing factor to disengagement in the school setting.

Case Study

Dewi is a 15-year-old student who had been excluded from two schools and, because of home circumstances, been placed with foster carers. Because of difficulties with anger management and due to frequent violent outbursts he had to be moved to new foster settings every few months. He had incredibly low self-esteem and found it difficult to establish positive relationships with peers and adults. A learning coach in his new school was attached to him and worked one-to-one with him, initially for several days each week.

The learning coach worked hard to develop rapport with Dewi and initially met with rejection. However she continued to work hard with him and through identifying the triggers to his anger and developing anger management strategies with him, she helped to reduce the number of anger episodes. She built his self-esteem by giving out praise and emotional small-change when he did well. She also identified difficulties he faced in numeracy and helped him understand key areas e.g. algebra, by breaking it down into bite-sized chunks.

Her work with Dewi was a roller-coaster ride but through perseverance, Dewi has now settled into his new school and foster setting, and is achieving well in school. He is establishing good relationships with adults and peers, and his anger outbursts are infrequent.

Factors that can lead to disaffection

Stressful lifestyles

Many young people have very stressful lifestyles which can lead to changes in behaviour. Gerhardt (2008) suggests that harsh, neglectful parenting and early separation from parent or attachment figure can play a significant part in the development of anti-social behaviour. Tremblay et al. (2004) state that young mothers who are unsupported by good personal relationships will fail to teach their children how to regulate their aggression. Gerhardt goes on to state that if a young person experiences undue stress in early years then cortisol, the stress hormone that is released, will have a toxic effect on the 'social brain' and can handicap its development which can lead to inappropriate interactions.

Mental health

These stressful experiences in early years together with other pressures throughout the school years can lead to some children suffering from Post-Traumatic Stress Disorder (PTSD). Up to 3 per cent of learners in classes may typically be suffering from this. This can lead to disengagement and often extreme responses to situations which are known as 'startle responses'.

The Good Childhood Inquiry (2008) found that over one million children aged 5–16 have a clinically recognized mental disorder ranging from depression, anxiety and anorexia to violent delinquency. The report stated that these mental health problems are occurring in increasing numbers and was described as a mental health epidemic. It discovered a growing proportion of UK children suffer from severe emotional and psychological distress. Girls are four times more likely than boys to suffer from eating disorders and to self-harm. Boys are four to five times more likely to attempt suicide. Two to four per cent of adolescents attempt suicide with 27 per cent of 13–15 year olds in England and Wales in a sample of 34,000 reporting that they have thought about taking their own lives in the past year (Survey by University of Newcastle 2003).

Food and drink

- Up to 17 per cent of learners arrive at school having eaten nothing for breakfast and 25 per cent arrive having just had sweets or crisps (Fuel for Thought (2004)).
- Too much processed food and additives are consumed which can impact on concentration and behaviour.
- Too little water is consumed and too many drinks that have a diuretic effect are taken. Water is a key part of the brain and is the basis of electrical firings in the brain.
- Food often lacks the necessary nutritional value.

Things that help:

- Taking fish oil supplements can help. When taking these students become less impulsive, their attention span increases and concentration and behaviour improve (Portwood 2004).
- Increasing zinc and iron in the diet and reducing sugar, chocolate, biscuits and soft drinks helped inmates of a Juvenile Offenders' Institution to reduce anti-social behaviour by 61 per cent over ten weeks (Northern 2004).

Crime

- Some learners become enmeshed in crime, particularly when they are connected with gangs. They have little respect for authority and see little point in education. They become disengaged with education and truant and abscond from schools. Over 70 per cent of offenders in the London area are under the age of 18 and for many of them, committing a crime means little – it is an unexceptional event.
- Many young offenders come from chaotic and sometimes abusive backgrounds.
- Children have not had the necessary moral guidance.

Addictions

Drugs

Greenfield (2007) reporting on NHS Information Centre research stated that:

- 11 per cent of 11–15 year olds use cigarettes.
- 22 per cent of 11–15 year olds use alcohol.
- 12 per cent of 11–15 year olds use cannabis.

- 7 per cent of 11–15 year olds use volatile substances such as glue.
- 4 per cent of 11–15 year olds use 'class A' drugs such as heroin.

Alcohol

- Binge drinking has reached new heights in teenagers, with those who drink regularly binge drinking on at least two days per week.
- Since 2000 there has been an 82.9 per cent rise in alcohol consumption in 11–13 year old girls. In boys it has risen 43.6 per cent (Viner 2007).

Gambling

- Some young people are more vulnerable to the negative effects of gambling such as becoming addicted to forms of gambling and stealing to enable gambling to take place.

Media

Many young people arrive at school disrupted by the powerful messages given to them by the media:

Television

- Too many violent images and extreme behaviour causes desensitization.
- Young people are unable to differentiate between fiction and reality.

Radio/Music

- There has been a rise in unsuitable lyrics and topics discussed on radio.

Magazines

- There is much unsuitable content aimed at younger age groups.

Internet

- Violent games desensitize students.
- Chatrooms encourage discussion of unsuitable topics.
- Lack of regulation of internet images and other content.

Computer games

- Watching violent video games affects brain chemistry which can limit an individual's capacity for empathy and sympathy.

- Adolescents who play violent games for just 30 minutes showed less activity in areas of the brain involved in inhibition, concentration and self-control (Indiana University School of Medicine 2007).

Schoolwork

The main issues are perceived as:

- work is not adapted/not differentiated enough
- work is not challenging or interesting
- poor relationship between teacher and student
- lack of trust or personality clash
- teacher stereotypes/labels students.

Steer (2005), in the report 'Learning Behaviour', noted with concern the disproportionately high level of exclusion of students with Special Educational Needs (SEN). Students with statements and SEN are four times more likely to be excluded from school. We see a close link between poor behaviour and previous failure to deal with a student's special needs properly. Many disaffected and disengaged students have not been appropriately supported and have not had their needs met.

Nurture

The behaviour of some disaffected students is such that staff feel that they are unable to modify this behaviour. Blakemore and Frith (2005) suggested that it is never too late for remedial care and nurture and that behaviours can be changed.

When talking about environmental deprivation they referred to babies found in orphanages in Romania following the fall of Ceaucescu. Many showed signs of autistic-like patterns of behaviour. It was found, however, that most babies made a full recovery by being placed in caring families with remedial stimulation. Schools can, through nurture, make a difference.

Gerhardt (2008) states that teachers can make a difference with the most difficult learners as children do a lot of emotional learning in school. Positive long-term care can make a difference. Blakemore suggests that individual brains like individual bodies are different from each other, but there is almost nothing that cannot improve or change. She suggests that education may be considered a kind of landscaping of the brain and educators are in a sense like gardeners. Given the number of disengaged and disaffected students with whom we work it is important that we remain positive and supportive; through the landscaping of their brains we help them to become successful learners.

The brain dimension

Sleep deprivation and poor diet have caused problems with learners' concentration and engagement in the classroom. NHS figures (2008) indicate that in the past five years there has been an increase of 26 per cent in the number of children referred to hospital for insomnia and other sleep-related disorders. Edinburgh Sleep Centre (2007) found that one in three youngsters in a survey of 1,000 12–16 year olds had just four to seven hours sleep per night instead of the recommended eight to nine hours. Televisions, DVDs, internet sites, chatrooms, video games, text messages and fast foods have left youngsters arriving at school moody, depressed and unable to concentrate.

Humans achieve maximum brain-cell density prior to birth. In the final months before birth, pruning of brain cells takes place. According to Dr Jay Giedd (chief of brain imaging at the National Institute of Mental Health) by the age of 6, a child's brain is 90–95 per cent of its adult size (cited in Wallis and Dell 2008). At this age another phase of pruning takes place which can lead to the onset of a number of syndromes and conditions, such as autism, which can be the result of insufficient or abnormal pruning. Giedd, quoted in Wallis and Dell (2008) states 'girls are about 11 and boys 12½, at which point a serious round of pruning is underway . . . [during adolescence] you get fewer but faster connections in the brain'.

The brain becomes more efficient but the individual loses some potential for learning and finds it difficult to recover from trauma. Wallis and Dell (2008) suggest that during the hormonal assault of puberty this phase of pruning is taking place, which leads to combustible emotions and unpredictable behaviour. This causes the disaffected behaviour many learners display in the classroom. Adolescents are looking for thrills and impulsive behaviour is likely. The thinking part of the brain, the pre-frontal cortex, is the part of the brain concerned with organization, prioritization and impulse suppression. During adolescence this part of the brain is smaller in size. To speed the development of this area of the brain we need to give learners real responsibility in the school environment and give them opportunities for cooperative learning (see Chapter 8).

 Top Tip

The sensory preference area of the brain is an area that develops first in the reconfiguring brain.

We all have at least one of these sensory preferences: the way that we take in and make sense of our environment.

- Visual – through sight. A visual learner usually watches the board intently and follows the teacher around with their eyes. A visual learner's eyes will frequently look upwards.

- Auditory – through hearing. An auditory learner turns their head slightly so their dominant ear is facing the presenter, nods their head in response to the teacher when they are speaking and repeats words to themselves. An auditory learner's eyes will frequently look straight ahead.
- Kinaesthetic – through movement and being tactile. A kinaesthetic learner fiddles with objects, clicking their pen and fidgeting with hands and feet. A kinaesthetic learner's eyes will frequently look down.
- Olfactory – through smell.
- Gustatory – through taste.

Often we can get an indication of a person's sensory preference by observing their eye movements.

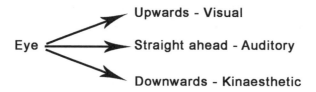

It is useful to listen to the words a learner uses when they are most upset or angry – often they will speak in the language of their sensory preference. To help support them and move them from an agitated state to a calmer state use matching responses by talking to them in the same language. For example, if a learner says 'I can't see the point', I would assume they are a visual learner and would reply using phrases such as 'It's clear to me' or 'I see what you mean'.

Key points

Key points to think about from this chapter are:

- the reasons why students arrive at school disrupted
- the causes of low self-esteem due to 'factory farming'
- the breakdown of the traditional family unit and disorderly homes leading to aggression
- the absence of role models and the contradictory messages students receive
- the importance of gangs and youth communities in young people's lives; their role as support networks and alternative families
- the connection between family break-up and the onset of emotional disorders
- the mental health of young people
- factors causing disaffection
- the brain dimension
- how emotional literacy and nurture can change behaviour and support brain development
- the use of sensory preferences to support disaffected students.

Using emotional literacy and impact techniques to raise self-esteem and resilience

2

In Chapter 1 we referred to education as being a landscaping of the brain and educators as like gardeners (Blakemore and Frith 2005). Students who are disengaged and disaffected need a lot of nurture, support and landscaping. According to Elias et al. (2001): 'Children enter school at different emotional starting places' (cited in Ciarrochi 2006). Because of the lack of emotional support some students do not have the emotional vocabulary to manage situations well and indeed they cannot decode the vocabulary being used by others. They are unable to read the body language of people around them or to display appropriate body language themselves. This can lead to challenging and difficult situations. As a result students turn into popular adolescent television characters and we have many Vicky Pollard, Lauren and Kevin moments. During adolescence many changes occur in the brain. Certain areas of the brain shrink back and give up their resources to allow other areas of the brain to develop. This leads to a massive period of pruning of brain cells. The pre-frontal cortex, which is the thinking part of the brain, is the area that suppresses impulses and is more risk-aversive. It is smaller in adolescents than in younger children. Winston (2003, p. 151) supports this, suggesting that the frontal lobes may reduce in puberty. 'It seems that an economic decision is made to put certain wiring circuits on hold so that more energy and attention can be given to the crucial purpose of creating a human adult ready for survival.' At this stage of development there is a lack of empathy and many adolescents are unable to display appropriate responses.

Self-esteem

Students can have incredibly low levels of self-esteem due to their experiences in education. The factory farming and testing culture (described in Chapter 1) make students feel inadequate and they perceive themselves as lacking ability. Many end up gaining kudos by misbehaving.

A student with low self-esteem may suffer from any or all of the following beliefs and behaviours:

- I am stupid and cannot learn.
- No-one likes me and I have no friends.
- I make negative comments about myself and believe that I am thick.
- I won't take risks or attempt tasks in case I look stupid.
- I often feel anxious.
- I find it difficult to talk to other students – I am withdrawn.
- I often lose my temper and blame others.

Long and Fogell (1999, p. 32) suggest that: 'Self-esteem is like oxygen. Children must have a good supply to thrive. Without it their behaviour can become frantic and dangerous if they "act out" or passive and withdrawn if they "act in".'

This is why it is essential for us to provide a secure, safe and positive environment for learners where we can give out 'emotional small-change' to students in the form of positive reinforcement and positive interactions.

In defining self-esteem Long and Fogell (1999, p. 33) state that self-esteem:

> refers to how much positive regard we feel towards ourselves. It is our evaluation of how far our self-image is from, or how close it is to, our ideal self . . . Children's self-esteem is clearly influenced by their experiences at both home and school . . . In school children need to have positive learning experiences and develop confidence and the motivation to learn. But, importantly, they need to feel accepted and valued.

It is important therefore to develop environments with a positive ethos where students feel valued and accepted. The table below outlines the qualities and characteristics in relation to low and high self-esteem in individuals. Many of the students we work with who are disaffected will have many of the characteristics of low self-esteem outlined in the table. It is our work to try and move learners from the low self-esteem end of the continuum to the high self-esteem end, for example from being limited communicators to good communicators.

High self-esteem	Low self-esteem
Good communicators.	Limited communication skills.
Clear vision.	Limited vision.
Clear short- and long-term goals.	Few or no goals of their own. Goals tend to be short. Unrealistic view of future.
Positive self-image.	Negative self-image.
Positive self-talk supported by a virtuous self-talk cycle.	Negative self-talk. Downward spiral of negative self-talk.
Successful risk takers.	Take few risks.
Wide comfort zones and able to expand zones.	Narrow comfort zones and unwilling to move outside their boundaries.
Have ownership of locus of control. 'I'm in charge.'	Locus of control lies outside self. Blame others.

Social and emotional aspects of learning

The Social and Emotional Aspects of Learning (SEAL) initiative, which has been introduced into primary and secondary schools as part of the National Strategy for School Improvement, addresses issues relating to emotional literacy. This has helped to increase students' self-awareness and raise self-esteem.

Primary SEAL was introduced in 2005 and further continued the work of promoting emotional and social skills that had been occurring for a long time in primary schools. Primary SEAL teaches these skills through a spiral curriculum with an assembly to start a theme, which is then studied in subjects and in a cross-curricular way. In the Social and Emotional Aspects of Learning for Secondary Schools (SEAL) guidance booklet (DfES 2007, p. 14) it states that a child leaving primary school at the end of Year 6 'will have experienced each key theme at an appropriate level each year, both at specific times during the school day and across all subject areas'.

Secondary SEAL (DfES 2007, p. 4) promotes social and emotional skills that 'underpin effective learning, positive behaviour, regular attendance . . . and the emotional health and well-being of all who learn and work in schools'. These skills help to develop positive relationships and help students to develop and manage their own emotions. They help individual students to understand and respond to the behaviour and emotions of others. If these skills are developed then students will be better motivated, will be successful learners, can be assertive and deal with conflict, can manage feelings, can work with others and develop friendships and understand differences between people.

The categorizing of these social and emotional skills is based on Goleman's (1996) five domains or components of emotional intelligence:

- self-awareness
- managing feelings
- motivation
- empathy
- social skills.

The SEAL strategy outlines ways that a school might teach the five domains across the curriculum. For example:

Managing feelings:

- consider how people feel as part of everyday discussions
- use everyday incidents to coach students in their responses
- teach students calming techniques.

How to develop empathy:

- storytelling
- demonstrate and model empathy
- promote tolerance and celebrate diversity.

How to develop social skills:

- encourage peer mediation and conflict resolution
- encourage cooperative learning and group projects.

The strategy also outlines how individual subjects might cover the five domains. By making effective use of the SEAL materials, schools are seeing the benefits of improved behaviour and the management of behaviour in students (see Further Reading).

Case Study

In a number of schools I have visited the school day has been restructured to develop emotional literacy and the SEAL strategy. On some or all school days the last lesson of the day, usually a short 30-minute period, is run in tutor groups where learners do work using SEAL materials, in order to develop their emotional literacy. Other schools give a learning theme to the session, for example 'Passport to Learning' where students look at ways of improving their learning and look at personalized learning, thinking skills and Goleman's five domains in relation to the SEAL project.

When emotional intelligence has been developed through various approaches students, particularly those who are disaffected:

- have a greater ownership of their locus of control
- are better communicators
- have a positive self-image
- have increased frustration tolerance
- have more assertiveness skills
- have greater empathy
- are less impulsive and have more self-control
- are better at resolving conflicts
- are more concerned.

Resilience

Some learners we meet come from complex and challenging environments and have had more than their share of life's difficulties thrown at them, and yet are quite resilient. Frieman (2001) suggests that characteristics such as personality, nature of the family and relationships they have with the community can impact directly on levels of resilience. He discusses, based on previous theory (see further Frieman 2001, pp. 10–11) that resilient children:

- have an optimistic view of life.
- feel independent
- feel that they have control over their environment
- have a sense of humour
- can empathize with others
- have effective problem-solving skills and coping strategies and have an internal locus of control.

It is interesting how these characteristics link with the qualities of high self-esteem students mentioned earlier in this chapter.

Case Study

One school in south-west England runs a re-tracking scheme for students who are disaffected and near to permanent exclusion. Several staff work with a group of eight to ten students over a half-term period. They follow a traditional timetable for some of the week, but for a few periods they have re-tracking sessions. In these sessions, staff work with the students in the following ways:

- social skills development with a member of staff
- support in key skills provided by additional needs staff
- a behaviour support worker helps students with anger management strategies

We stated in Chapter 1 that the cause of disaffection and problem behaviours is the lack of appropriate parenting, modelling and shaping of appropriate behaviour in early years. Many of the students who show disaffection and behavioural difficulties have had a lack of guidance and support from parents. Frieman (2001) suggests the importance of having a key parental figure, particularly in the child's first year. The family characteristics of resilient children in the period up to the first year at school are:

- parents who are competent, loving and patient
- child has a good relationship with at least one parental figure
- alternative caretakers step in when parents are absent
- there is little separation from the primary caretaker during the first year.

Networks of friends (see further Frieman 2001, p. 11), community members including religious leaders and neighbours also play a significant part in guiding and supporting these children and helping them become more resilient. The role of teaching staff in the development of resilience should not be underestimated. They can do this by creating a positive classroom atmosphere where everyone is mutually supportive and everyone feels psychologically safe and where staff help learners to solve the problems.

Teachers also have an immensely important role as they model appropriate behaviour which students notice. To help children to become resilient teachers need to:

- be themselves most of the time
- be aware of their own feelings and reactions to situations
- be an encourager
- have positive attitudes to students – show interest, respect and warmth
- enter the map of each student's world (see Chapter 3 – Neuro-Linguistic Programming)
- be consistent
- be dependable
- be trustworthy
- be a listener and care for student opinion
- be forgiving.

Impact techniques

Impact techniques are multisensory interventions that make abstract concepts more concrete through the use of images, movements, objects and language. They help students to decode information through intuition and experience. They can help students to manage attitude or behaviour problems and can in particular develop self-control, empathy and motivation. Many of the techniques help to develop a student's emotional intelligence.

Impact techniques exploit current understanding of the brain, learning and memory function. By understanding and utilizing them in the classroom, you will have a significant impact on learners. They are based on 'impact therapy', a multi-sensory approach to therapy which was developed by Dr Ed Jacobs of West Virginia University (see Beaulieu 2006).

Danie Beaulieu (2004) has carried out some very interesting work on how impact techniques can be used in the classroom environment to engage disaffected students. She suggests (2004, p. 17) using impact techniques are like 'giving your teaching efforts a sort of learning amplifier which multiplies the anchors in the students' minds, allowing them to integrate new knowledge (whether intellectual or emotional) more quickly, more deeply and with greater intensity'.

Beaulieu highlights the importance of a multisensory approach in the classroom rather than just focusing on verbal communications. She suggests (2004, p. 17) the underlying principle with impact techniques is that they 'appeal to many senses, the information that they transmit lodges in several areas of the brain and constitutes a global message that is loaded with possibilities for recall'.

When faced with disaffected students, we should consider what strategies we can make use of to actively engage students in the learning process. Beaulieu (2004) suggests several key strategies we can incorporate with impact techniques including the use of images, developing short lessons, use of repetition and moving from the known to the unknown. One specific technique suggested by Beaulieu is the 'Worry Jar' technique – where students are encouraged to write down their worries on slips of paper and then put them in a jar. The worries stay in the jar until the end of the lesson when they can be collected. This technique, among many others outlined in Beaulieu's book *Impact Techniques in the Classroom* (2004), are extremely effective when used with disengaged and disaffected students.

Storytelling and metaphors

This area links well with a number of the impact technique approaches. Storytelling and metaphors are good strategies to use to support students and to develop emotional literacy. By using story you can develop a character with the same first name as the student experiencing similar situations. Through story you can reflect upon actions taken by the individual. You can reflect upon appropriate and inappropriate actions. Through the use of metaphors you can also project a problem onto someone else, or a place or object. Faupel et al. suggest (1998, p. 67) that:

> If a 'dangerous' story is retold in a more solution-focused way, using metaphor, then many children with problem anger can be more open to the indirect messages than simply being told how better to respond or behave.

The mutual storytelling technique works with children with conduct disorders who do not have a sense of guilt about their behaviour. A child chooses an object and then tells a story about it. Faupel (1998, p. 67) says:

> Storytelling can enable the child to reframe guilt into a more positive emotion, by developing, instead a sense of remorse, whilst at the same time exploring how the child might use this sense of remorse to avoid problem anger in the future.

Case Study

One Pupil Referral Unit (PRU) in the Midlands encourages learners to produce puppets from various resources (including scrap card and cloth). These puppets are given a name by the student and they use them to project or displace their problem. The puppet is able to talk about the problem in a way that the student would not be able to. Staff also sometimes use a puppet when discussing the issues with the student's puppet. This strategy has been very helpful in unburdening students, particularly the stuffers who hide their worries or concerns.

Transactional analysis

We use transactional analysis (TA) techniques frequently in our work with learners without often being aware of it. Transactional analysis techniques are particularly needed with students who are disaffected or have social, emotional and behavioural difficulties. Transactional analysis is a model relating to people and relationships that was developed by Dr Eric Berne during the 1960s. It is based on two notions:

(i)   We have three ego states to our personality.
(ii) These ego states converse with one another in transaction.

It develops explanations of how we continue to use strategies developed in early childhood throughout life even when these produce outcomes that are self-defeating. Many actions and behaviours result from childhood memories stored in the hippo-campus area of the brain. If students experience turbulent and traumatic events in early life the high levels of the stress hormones released (cortisol, adrenalin) results in the hippocampus being flooded and the memories being stored at a subconscious level (see Chapter 10 for more information on this). When a new event stimulates the release of the stress hormone cortisol then the deep-seated memory is released. This can cause extreme and childlike behaviours even in adults. This is a life script, a way to respond to situations which is often at a subconscious level.

Key ideas and areas in transactional analysis are:

- ego state model
- transactions and strokes
- autonomy

Ego states

Human personality is made up of three ego states. Each ego state is an entire system of thoughts, feelings and behaviours which interact with one another. It is a way in which we manifest a part of our personality at a given time. Transactional analysis portrays three ego states:

- adult – behaving, thinking, feeling in response to what is going on around me in the here and now
- parent – behaving, thinking, feeling in ways that are a copy of one of my parents
- child – behaving, thinking, feeling how I used to when I was a child.

Transactions and strokes

Transactions refer to communication exchanges between two people. For example I could address you from any of my ego states and you could reply in turn from any ego state. This exchange is called a transaction. The use of the ego state model to analyse sequences of transactions is transactional analysis. For example, when two people 'transact', one person will signal recognition of the other person who will most likely return that recognition – any act of recognition is a stroke. People need strokes, the units of interpersonal recognition to survive, thrive and to maintain their well-being. Understanding how people give and receive positive and negative strokes and changing unhealthy patterns of stroking are powerful aspects of transactional analysis. Transactional analysts are trained to recognize which ego states people are transacting from and to, and follow the transactional sequences so that they can intervene and improve the quality and effectiveness of communication.

In interactions with challenging and disaffected students we should try to identify the ego state they are in and choose an appropriate state to adopt. In the adult world a male with 'man flu' may be in a child ego state. Their partner, to manage the situation may adopt the parent ego state which helps the male feel nurtured.

There are four key areas of strokes; three areas represent positive and developmental stokes – approval, acceptance and those that set expectations. The other area is characterized by negative or 'scorpion' strokes, which reject the person.

Hearts	Diamonds
Acceptance strokes: • show appreciation of the person • give acceptance for who you are and how you are feeling.	**Approval strokes:** • show appreciation for what the person has done well • show approval for behaviours that you've shown.
Spades	Clubs

Strokes to set expectations and set limits on poor performance:
• coaching in advance/ coaching to correct mistakes
  ○ strokes to set expectations and give explanations for how to do well
  ○ to give help and support.
• Stokes to set limits on poor performance and to implement a tough mentoring process.
	Strokes which reject the person:
	• hidden or disguised hurtfulness – scorpion strokes
	• overt put-downs
	  ○ snubs
	  ○ negative name-calling.

(Based on the work of Gradous 1990.)

Gradous (1990) suggested that acceptance and approval strokes are needed in large quantities particularly when working with disaffected students. Acceptance strokes give appreciation of the person and acceptance for how they are feeling.

Approval strokes give approval for what the person has done well and for their behaviours. When using positive strokes we need to avoid using non-genuine plastic strokes. In coaching and supporting students we also need to use strokes that set expectations and give help and support. We can do this by coaching in advance or to correct mistakes by identifying a problem and agreeing solutions. The strokes we need to avoid totally are those that reject the person by put-downs and by using 'scorpion strokes' which are negative and hurtful.

 Top Tip

Keep it positive – in our interactions with students it is not possible to give too many positive strokes. Give approval strokes for good behaviour and for what the student has done well. Give acceptance strokes to show appreciation for them as a person and how they are feeling.

Autonomy

Transactional analysis helps people achieve autonomy, to move away from life scripts we carry and to update our strategies to the way we approach life which are in keeping with the here and now and not the life scripts we carry from our childhood. With autonomy we develop the capacity for spontaneity and awareness.

Positive entrapment

It is important to move disengaged learners from the cycle of negative entrapment that they are in – they can 'awfulize' and be quite negative about their position. Students are often negative to help insulate themselves from the negative feedback they continually get.

Some ways of developing a positive outlook in students are:

- Setting up a positive learning environment (refer to Chapter 5).
- Using one-to-one working.
- Setting short-term targets: chunk down the learning so that they can achieve early success and instant gratification.
- Giving out nuggets of praise or emotional small-change whenever you can.
- Showing frequent approval of the individual – verbally or non-verbally.
- Using circle time strategies and share time.
- Using role play and activities to develop assertiveness.
- Using materials to develop their emotional vocabulary. For example 'Toon Cards', which consist of 120 cards with cartoon images relating to phrases on behaviour, feelings and qualities (40 on each). Some activities include: emotional stepping stones, where 120 Toon Cards are laid face up across the floor and students walk across them stepping on the cards that relate to them; emotional dominoes, played

in groups where students have a number of Toon Cards and they lay the cards down in turn and justify how the phrase on their card can be connected to the last card; circle time involves one student sitting in the centre of a circle of students with each student handing the student in the centre a Toon Card that relates to a positive quality, feeling or behaviour that they have. (Toon Cards are published by Network/Continuum and can be purchased from www.continuumbooks.com.)

- Using a solution-focused approach – working one-to-one:
  - get the students to look for signs of improvement and get them to identify when things go well
  - get them to ask the miracle question – if a miracle occurs and problems we are working on go away how will it show it is better tomorrow? What will have changed?
- Using relaxation techniques. Get students to lie on the floor and tense and relax muscles in the body starting with toes, ankles, calf muscles, buttocks, stomach, arms, shoulders and neck. They could also use controlled breathing – breathing in through the nose on a count of four, holding breath for a count of three and exhaling through the mouth on a count of four, repeating 20 times.
- Using visualization techniques by getting them to close their eyes and visualize a special location and at the same time use controlled breathing.
- Getting students to identify their worries or concerns and letting them drift away. Ask them to lie on the floor and relax, breathing with their eyes closed and ask them to imagine that they have been given a number of helium-filled balloons, each with a label on, to hold. Ask them to write a different worry they may have on each label – then in turn let each balloon go blowing upwards as it is released.
- Develop positive thinking – including coping thoughts.
- Using humour.
- Using an emotion diary – recording when they are angry, sad, happy.
- Head massages.
- Giving star shapes to students on which they can record what they will be in five years time. What will they look like? Will they be in training or education or employment? They can compare themselves with other students in a positive way. There must be a positive theme to stars.

The way we support learners and help to develop their emotional literacy will have a significant impact on them and if done successfully they are more likely to feel positive about themselves and engage. The behaviour we model is key, as Professor Eric Jensen suggested: 'Your success as an educator is more dependent on positive, caring, trustworthy relationships than any skill, idea, tip or tool.'

Case Study

In a primary school in the south of England staff help students who have had a bad day or poor break time by putting them through the 'emotional car wash' – the student pretends to be a car and friends gently pat them on the back as they go through an imaginary car wash. This school also trains students in head massage and students spend some time each week head massaging each other.

For both these activities parental permission is sought. Also health and safety issues have to be considered in relation to head massage – particularly in relation to using a hygienic hand wash and precautions relating to head lice need to be taken.

Key points

Key points to think about from this chapter are:

- the importance of self-esteem and how to raise the self-esteem of learners
- social and emotional aspects of learning
- the benefits of developing emotional literacy
- characteristics of resilient students and how this resilience can be developed
- the use of impact techniques to engage disaffected students
- the powerful effect of storytelling
- using transactional analysis
- developing positive entrapment.

3 Using Neuro-Linguistic Programming (NLP) to successfully manage disaffected students

The way disaffected students communicate can lead to difficulties. They find it difficult to develop positive relationships and can be confrontational. They often have not been taught how to communicate their feelings effectively. In some families little conversation occurs and they do not experience modelling of appropriate behaviours and methods of communicating.

Developing Neuro-Linguistic Programming (NLP) strategies and approaches can be helpful in giving students confidence in communication and helping staff to read situations and to develop rapport with learners. NLP is a way of communicating that helps us in our day-to-day lives. In particular it improves our effectiveness in communication. It was developed in the 1970s by Richard Bandler and John Grinder (a psychologist and linguist respectively). Mahony (2007, p. ix) states that NLP 'is a model of human communication and behaviour . . . It is ideally suited for managing classroom behaviour'.

He suggests that it is made up of three elements:

- building rapport and communicating with others
- gathering information about another person's view of the world
- promotion of behaviour-change strategies.

Key components of NLP

The concept of NLP has many key components which are important to consider in the classroom environment as well as in day-to-day life:

- understanding yourself and understanding others
- attitude is important – respecting others, reassuring them if necessary
- recognizing others' uniqueness is of utmost importance
- understanding how to build rapport with others
- try to draw the unique map of the world that each individual inhabits. It will be a unique map – attempt to enter their world
- understanding your own and others' anchors – anchors are positive or negative memories associated with senses – For example:
  - **smell** – the smell of baking bread could bring back positive memories from being young and in the kitchen with your parents
  - **hearing** – a piece of music from adolescence engages the nostalgia bump in the brain and brings back happy memories from those days.
- Anchoring a disaffected student into a positive memory by identifying these positive anchors and getting the student to engage with them will help.
- Developing listening skills – deep listening rather than cosmetic is important. Try this when you first meet someone and introduce yourself and ask a general question. Avoid 'me, me, me' moments, where you swamp the person with facts and information about yourself.
- Managing distortions, deletions and generalizations that are made. People use language in a variety of ways. Distortions are when the meaning of the experience is altered. Deletions are when people describing an incident miss out key points. Generalizations occur when logic is presented in an illogical manner through generalizing. By listening to the way people say things and 'listening between the lines' (Miller 2008, p. 80) we can get additional information.
- Developing the ability to read body language and project positive body language yourself.
- Understanding how to reframe positively. Many people will 'awfulize' and focus on the negativities surrounding their lives. Reframing is getting people to view things positively.

The essence of NLP is about understanding the person you are communicating with. It is nicely described by Miller (2008, p. 12), who suggests 'it's about understanding yourself and it's about the understanding between you and other people'. In any classroom environment we need to make sure there are no misunderstandings in the way we communicate.

 Top Tips

- Develop active listening skills – try to understand as much as you can about the student by listening carefully to them.
- Try to identify what is really being said. Learners will generalize, distort the message and will delete or miss things out.
- Anchor the student if they are distressed. Get them to refer to a positive or happy memory as this will change their mood.

In order to avoid any misunderstandings in the classroom we need to be careful with the language we use. Mahony (2007) suggests that through carefully choosing our language we can 'actively create mental images and neuro-logical pathways in the brain of the child to produce the desired learning' (p. x). According to Mahony 'specific language patterns, vocabulary and ways of talking' (ibid.) can cause an emotional shift for the listener, which can lead to better behaviour in students.

If we look at a typical classroom environment, choosing specific language patterns can lead to positive behaviour from the student. Carefully choosing our vocabulary by using sensory predicates (talking in the language of the sensory preference of the student) we can move them to a calmer emotional state (see Top Tip in Chapter 1, p. 7–8).

Accelerated learning

NLP techniques in the classroom form an important part of accelerated learning – a technique which promotes effective learning based on brain research, and strategies to support the learner. Some of the key areas considered in accelerated learning are:

- the emotional and physical state of the learner (as discussed earlier in Chapter 1)
- a multisensory approach to learning (involving as many of the senses as possible e.g. visual, auditory, kinaesthetic, olfactory and gustatory)
- impact of music on learning and brain state
- brain breaks and physical activities (this will be discussed later in Chapter 8)
- developing positive learning environments
- working to create positive relationships and good rapport
- helping learners to understand their individual learner profiles
- the importance of rehydration and appropriate diet

- clear sequences of sessions and provision of activities accessible to all students
- developing learning skills and memory techniques.

Using NLP approaches will help to engage the disaffected. Good working relationships are essential with students and developing rapport (making a two-way connection with another person or group) with them is essential. It is important to establish rapport before expecting them to listen to you. Developing rapport relies on watching, listening and attempting to understand the person and their intentions. When you meet someone try to find some common ground or interests – the 'like likes like' theory. Tune into them and their interests. Become an active listener and understand their context. Try to develop two-way understanding or two-way traffic. Boothman (2000, p. 19) states that 'Rapport is the lubricant that allows social exchanges to flow smoothly'. It is important to be authentic. Develop empathy and try to be engaging. When meeting someone initially it is important to develop empathy; if you are insincere it will show, with plastic body language and plastic verbal strokes. Keep it real. Students are very good at spotting signs of weakness. With disaffected and disengaged students you should avoid any incongruence – where verbal and non-verbal communication are in conflict. Often staff can talk firmly but have weak body language or vice versa. We need to be congruent in our communication by using firm body language and talking in a firm confident manner. Boothman (p. 13) suggests that 'the key to establish rapport . . . is to learn how to become like them'.

Mirror neurones are thought to be responsible for the importance and success of rapport building. Churches and Terry (2007, p. 23) state that: 'The human brain is thought to have multiple mirror neurone systems that enable us not only to understand the actions of others but also their intentions, emotions and the social meaning of their behaviours.'

If you mirror or match another person's body language and style of vocal delivery you can give them a feeling of being understood. This is creating rapport. Mirroring and matching are key skills to use to develop rapport. Churches and Terry (p. 25) go on to suggest that 'we can create rapport by matching and mirroring another person's body language and voice tonality by joining their dance. This creates a bridge between our world and theirs. This builds trust and is the basis of effective communication.'

It is important to remember how we project ourselves – particularly in relation to our attitude.

Case Study

NLP teaching and learning with performing arts techniques

At the Harris Academy in Peckham, south-east London, they run two unique programmes:

- A Level 2 certificate in Peer Coaching and Learning with NLP
- A Level 3/4 certificate in NLP Teaching and Learning with Performing Arts.

The NLP will benefit students, teachers and support staff by enhancing their communication skills (e.g. rapport), their varied use of questioning techniques and their ability to deal with and resolve conflict amicably.

Ray Lau, curriculum coordinator for performing arts (with responsibility for the Specialism) describes the scheme in more detail:

'The Level 2 certificate in Peer Coaching and Learning with NLP is currently in pilot mode targeting Year 9 and above students. This enables not only personalized learning but developing student leadership and voice within the academy. Volunteers are selected and are trained in developing their knowledge and awareness of strategies in learning, enhancing their communication skills including developing their rapport skills and ability to use eye-accessing cues. Students will develop their use of language and questioning tools to help them coach other peers using selected but relevant NLP techniques such as perceptual positions when dealing with conflict.

The Level 3/4 certificate in Teaching and Learning with Performing Arts is designed for both teachers and support staff to raise standards across the academy. Our specialism performing arts status requires impact of the performing arts subjects across the institution. I had completed practitioner and coach practitioner courses in NLP and have gone on to develop a course where colleagues can, in specific modules in music, drama and dance access and use NLP techniques with students in these curricular areas. We are currently coaching individual staff interested in these techniques. The key was keeping the programme very flexible, which has enabled those interested in NLP to complete the Diploma in Education with Inner Sense, a registered NLP provider. People then also complete the coaching module so they can gain further accreditation. This has attracted interest within our local primary schools and I have presented this at a teaching and learning conference at the South London Harris Federation of Academies.'

When meeting someone for the first time you should observe key aspects of their body language including gestures, mannerisms, posture and vocal delivery. When you have completed your detective work, you will probably notice some of the key rapport building strategies you can use. They must work because they are in every salesperson's manual of ways to make a sale!

Some of the key elements requiring consideration in building rapport are discussed over the next few pages.

Body language

Keeping body language open, not closed

When you meet someone you should avoid developing closed body language and barrier positions. For example, do not have folded arms or stand behind a barrier such as a table. Avoid holding objects such as books to your chest. Open your arms, show your palms and stand in open space away from barriers.

Matching body language

This is copying another person's body language and behaviour. If someone is talking with their left hand touching their chin then to match this we should stand and hold our left hand to our chin.

Mirroring body language

Here you adopt a mirror image – this time if their left hand is on their chin you put your right hand to your chin. The other person sees the image as though they are looking in a mirror. Their thought might be 'They look like me, therefore I like them'.

Cross-over matching

You identify a behaviour usually by observing the rate at which someone does something (e.g. the breathing or blinking rate). You then match this rate with a behaviour of your own. For example, hand or foot tapping.

Matching gestures

Try to identify and match some of the following gestures:

- hand movements
- feet tapping
- head tilts and movements

- facial expressions
- cycle of eye contact and eye movements
- breathing – similar speed, depth, match breathing pattern
- body shifts
- posture including spine angle.

Try practising interactional synchronizing where we attempt to move in a similar way.

Speech

Try some of these techniques:

- use same sentence length
- similar rhythm and intonation
- match descriptive words
- match key phrases and exact words
- copy repetitive phrasing
- use similar colloquialisms
- discover the sensory predicates they use and match them. Often people will be strong in one sensory preference, for example visual, auditory or kinaesthetic. Match in the same proportion the predicates they use. The Top Tip at the end of Chapter 1 describes sensory predicates in more detail.
- Find commonality of interest.
- Match their use of silence.

Vocal matching

Vocal matching is a key element of developing rapport with another person:

- vocal sounds
- volume
- pitch
- tempo
- rhythm and tonality
- speech patterns.

Emotional rapport

Identify the person's emotional state and try to establish emotional rapport. If a student is angry do not respond by being quiet and low key. Match them with the same voice volume and tone and speed. Also make statements to show that you can see their strength of feeling. A number of strategies to help students to manage their own behaviour are given in Chapter 9.

Building group rapport

Building rapport within the group can be very important with challenging, disaffected and disengaged students. By doing activities together as a class we can build group rapport. We can also use these activities to discover the leaders in the class, often the alpha males and females. When using brain breaks with a whole group, no individual will do the activity until the ringleader does it. They are often called the rapport leader. Spotting these leaders is key in the management of behaviour. Once identified we should use a range of rapport building strategies with them. Some activities we can use to develop class rapport are:

- brain breaks (see Chapter 8 for examples of these), which synchronize movement
- maintaining eye contact with the whole group by standing in a position in the room where you can lighthouse the whole group
- the scripts you use – truisms – 'We are all ready to start', 'We are all nearly finished'
- asking questions to which the majority could answer yes and getting the group to raise their hand whilst simultaneously doing so yourself
- using props arms or smiling faces (as will be discussed in Chapter 7) where the whole group uses theirs at the same time
- using sound effects, a samba whistle or a piece of music to which the group could clap along.

Pacing and leading to build rapport

Pacing and leading are key ways of influencing students. You will know if you have been successful in building rapport with people as they will be more open to suggestions – you will find it easier to lead them. Pacing is about really listening to a person and understanding where they are coming from. Whilst pacing you build rapport by picking up and matching their body language, behaviours and vocabulary. Leading is when you subtly take them in a new direction.

Ready and Burton (2004) use the metaphor of pacing being like running alongside a train and waiting until your speed matches the train, before taking a leap to jump on. If you tried jumping on straight away you would fall off.

As well as these strategies, there are other ways you can build rapport:

- be interested in them
- hold brief informal conversation
- discover something that you have in common
- use positive labels – 'I need someone with a good memory'.

Mismatching

It is important to identify when people are not getting on. Mismatching occurs when body posture, orientation and gestures show a lack of synchronization. Often people will be stood looking away from each other with their arms folded. If you are working with a disaffected student then they may adopt similar body language. Trying to break the negative body language is key. Changing our position may be useful. Psychological geography can be helpful where we stand alongside a person rather than facing them. Standing close to their 50cm space bubble (a comfort zone which surrounds us all) can create a more positive feeling. Chapter 8 contains some useful brain breaks which can be used to break the barriers.

Breaking rapport

It is important sometimes for us to be able to break rapport, for example by changing our position by looking at our watch or by moving towards the door.

This chapter has looked at the importance of NLP and establishing rapport with learners to create a positive relationship and to help us to connect with them. It is important to note, however that for some students with certain syndromes and conditions, it is almost impossible for them to read body language in others and so some of these strategies would not work. Alternative approaches to use are given in later chapters in the book.

Key points

Key points to think about from this chapter are:

- the key components of NLP
- the language we should use with learners – the importance of sensory predicates
- anchoring a disaffected student into a positive memory
- understanding that when students speak they can generalize, distort and delete key points
- the link between NLP and accelerated learning
- the key skills needed to develop rapport with learners
- using accelerated learning techniques with students.

4 Syndromes and conditions

A total of 1.9 million children, nearly one in five, in England and Wales are considered by their school to have special educational needs (SEN) (Audit Commission 2002). The numbers of students with conditions and syndromes appears to be increasing. Turbulent lifestyles, aggressive home life and additive-fuelled diets have all contributed to the increase. With Attention Deficit Hyperactivity Disorder (ADHD), common environmental factors such as poverty, family lifestyle, pollution or diet account for 30 per cent of all cases. A number of the conditions are more likely to occur in boys. For example, autistic boys outnumber autistic girls between three and four to one.

An absence of spindle cells, which develop about four months after birth, can cause developmental delays and Autistic Spectrum Disorders. Under-functioning spindle cells cause Attention Deficit Disorder (ADD) and Attention Deficit Hyperactivity Disorder (ADHD). Reasons for an absence of or lower levels of spindle cells are: genetic factors; high oestrogen levels during pregnancy, which affects the male brain whilst the female brain is unaffected; a diet high in E-numbers and too much sugar and salt. Excluding or reducing these factors in the diet will lead to an immediate improvement in behaviour; diet should include essential fatty acids and nutrients.

If development of spindle cells is impeded then one area of the brain can under-function, which in turn causes another area to under-function. This is called diaschisis – one area of the brain doesn't work well because the area it normally communicates with has a problem. Brain exercise through brain breaks helps to open up neural pathways to these under-functioning areas of the brain.

As the nervous system is not developed until late teens a balanced diet is needed to help with the development and functioning of nerve fibres. Adolescents often demand inappropriate foods, which trigger 'the pleasure centre' of the brain. These foods can damage or delay the developing spindle cells. Stabilizers and colourants, including aspartame used in drinks, can lead to large amounts of glutamate (an excitatory neurotransmitter) to be released resulting in hyperactivity and poor behaviour.

In this chapter we will look at a range of syndromes and conditions and identify the signs that indicate that a student could have the condition. We will look at likely causes and the strategies that could be used in the classroom to support learners with these syndromes and conditions. Early intervention and treatment of developmental disorders, in which children do not develop at the normal rate, can help students develop skills and achieve their best potential.

The following conditions are covered:

- Attention Deficit Hyperactivity Disorder (ADHD)
- Autistic Spectrum Disorders: Asperger Syndrome (AS)
- Dyslexic cluster: dyslexia, dysgraphia, dyscalculia and dyspraxia
- Other conditions: Tourette's Syndrome (TS), Conduct Disorder (CD) and Pathological Demand Avoidance syndrome (PDA).

Vizard and Vizard (2007b) have written extensively on a range of syndromes and conditions.

Attention Deficit Hyperactivity Disorder (ADHD)

Students who have this developmental disorder usually have emotional and behavioural difficulties; the main categories are hyperactivity, impulsivity and inattention. A typical student with ADHD will have difficulties concentrating, will find it hard to follow instructions, will have trouble organizing activities and will be continually 'on the go' – always talking and fidgeting. They will often shout out answers, have difficulty in waiting their turn and often interrupt or join conversations without invitation. Potential causes of ADHD include brain abnormalities, brain injury or trauma, environmental factors and hereditary factors.

Strategies to use with students who have ADHD

Classroom environment

- Minimize distractions. By using soundproofing on walls and carpets noise levels will be reduced.
- Sitting students near to windows where they can look out or by main aisles in classrooms will be a big distractor. Move them away from busy spots.

Structure of the lesson

- Keep it simple and predictable. Keep seating arrangements, rules, expectations and logical consequences consistent.
- Provide structure; start the day with a mentor-led planning session.
- Have the same subject occuring at the same time each day.
- Try to keep a specific desk in each classroom assigned to the student. If possible the student should remain in the same location.
- Develop organizational skills in the student.

Instructions given in the classroom

- when speaking and giving instructions to a student, call out their first name
- use short sentences
- repeat instructions
- maintain eye contact
- repeat rules if needed
- keep tasks varied
- break up tasks into easy to manage steps so that they can see an obtainable end to their work.

Behaviour expectation and management

- Make behaviour expectations clear.
- If a student misreads a situation, help them to understand what happened and give them strategies to use in the future. In relation to impulsivity, encourage students to write down their thoughts and ideas and get the teacher to discuss these with them later.
- Behaviour systems need to reflect positive and negative performance.

Rewards and sanctions to use with ADHD students

- Children with ADHD need to be rewarded and disciplined immediately.
- Make boundaries of acceptable and unacceptable behaviour clear, and reward or sanction as required.
- Use whole-class rewards to ensure peer support.
- Avoid public criticism but praise positive behaviour.
- Do not become confrontational – children with ADHD respond best to calmness.

Study skills to develop with ADHD students

- Develop study skills. For example typing, use of laptop and calculators.

Support needed by ADHD students

- Create an appropriate support team, including healthcare professional, family and friends, educational professionals and members of the community.

- Provide specialist reinforcement in reading, writing, spelling and speaking.
- Make use of mentoring, coaching and counselling.
- Consider nurture groups – this can help with self-esteem, relationships, interactions, academic expectations, and talking about issues such as lying and stealing.
- Provide frequent one-to-one feedback and personal contact.
- Avoid trying to single out a student with ADHD and avoid giving them too much attention as they will not want to look needy.

Use of ICT

- teach typing, laptop and calculator skills
- make use of headphones to block out external sounds.

Case Study

In schools in the Durham area learners have the opportunity to take fish oil supplements during the school day. Findings suggest that after a period of three months, students were less impulsive, their behaviour improved, they were calmer and brainpower was improved. Also for some students with ADHD the fish oil supplements improved their behaviour and as a result some of these students no longer needed their medication.

Case Study

In one young offenders' institution, the diets of inmates were adapted. Previously they had a diet rich in sugar, chocolate, biscuits and soft drinks. This diet was changed so that they had a reduced level of these food and drink items. They were also given an increased level of zinc and iron (currently school students only get 80 per cent of the iron they need and 70 per cent of the recommended amount of zinc). Within ten weeks of the diet change there was a sharp reduction in anti-social behaviour by up to 61 per cent. Dietary changes together with classroom activities such as brain breaks have led to increased levels of concentration, motivation, academic achievement and improved behaviour. Changes in diet can have a significant impact on certain syndromes and conditions.

Autistic Spectrum Disorders

Disorders in this spectrum affect learners in many different ways, such as their ability to communicate with others and relate to the world. Some learners who have severe autism are unable to communicate and feel cut off. Others can be high functioning and are high academic achievers but are socially cut off.

Asperger's Syndrome (AS)

Asperger Syndrome (AS) is one of the Autistic Spectrum Disorders and it is characterized by difficulty with social interaction such as communication, socialization and imagination. Sometimes physical coordination is also a problem. Restricted and repetitive patterns of behaviour, interests and activities develop. A student with Asperger Syndrome finds it difficult to:

- read non-verbal communication in others
- have empathy with others
- be able to sustain eye contact.

Because of their lack of social skills they are often prone to being bullied and find it hard to join in with discussions or activities. When faced with challenge a student with Asperger Syndrome may take flight and run off or vent their frustration in a temper tantrum. They can be over-precise and jokes and metaphors can be interpreted in the wrong way. Because of their need for routine, timetable or staff changes can cause anxiety. They may have mood disorders such as anxiety or depression. Potential causes of Asperger Syndrome include brain structure, low levels of serotonin and allergic reactions, and it is thought to have a genetic link, although these potential causes have yet to be conclusively proved.

Strategies to use with students who have Asperger Syndrome

Stress-relief techniques

- To help students avoid becoming stressed, use a pictorial representation of the timetable to help them with establishing a routine.
- Teach students relaxation techniques to help them feel calm. Breathing exercises and stress balls can be used.
- Be aware of high levels of stress or depression and provide someone to whom they can speak.
- When anxious or worried allow time out in a safe zone.

Establish clear routines and structures

- Build up routines that are in the student's best interest while breaking down routines that tend to be destructive.
- Ensure the students have a clear copy of their timetable at all times and know where to go for a replacement.

Create an appropriate environment

- Keep it the same – ensure that there is predictability to the environment.
- Ensure students know of any room changes or a change of teacher or teaching assistant well in advance.

Appropriate use of language

- Instructions and the language used should be clear. Avoid ambiguity, humour or irony. For example do not use expressions such as 'It's raining cats and dogs' or 'My feet are killing me'. This will cause confusion. Language should be simple and literal. For example 'Sit down, please'.

Ways to build self-esteem

- Give positive feedback whenever possible.
- Rehearse with the students what to do in different situations. For example, explain to them how to react if they are teased.

Utilize visual stimuli

- Make use of visual props as visual information is better absorbed than auditory information.
- Use pictures and photographs of people displaying different emotions and get students to identify their feelings.

Ways to develop social skills

- Develop different strategies to improve their social skills.
- Encourage cooperative behaviour, such as turn taking, fairness and not always winning.

The importance of diet

- Although there is relatively little theory supporting this, choice of diet may help control symptoms. For example:
  - a gluten-free diet can help reduce behavioural problems
  - fish oils – the fatty acids found in these can improve concentration.
- However, a potential side effect of changing the diet of a child with AS is the anxiety it may cause. Banning certain foods can result in this. Therefore careful consideration should be taken when adopting such a strategy.

Other strategies that may be useful

- Provide break-time supervision as this unsupervised time is when they are most vulnerable.
- Cognitive Behavioural Therapy (CBT) can help the student in managing emotions and controlling symptoms associated with Asperger Syndrome.

Dyslexic cluster

These are a group of learning difficulties which are closely related and result in difficulties in reading (dyslexia), in writing (dysgraphia), in mathematics (dyscalculia) and in coordination (dyspraxia).

Dyslexia

Dyslexia affects the way the brain processes written material. Dyslexia can either be acquired as a result of an illness or accident, or developmental. Characteristics vary from person to person but a common trait is that people with dyslexia read at levels significantly lower than typical for people of their age and intelligence.

Dyslexia usually causes problems with a student's spelling, writing, organization, memory, speech and processing of information. Other signs that can sometimes be seen in dyslexic students are poor concentration, low self-esteem and hyperactivity. The cause is thought to be due to genetic make-up. Patterns of brain activity and neural connections are different in dyslexics.

Strategies to use with students who have dyslexia

Develop the art of proofreading

- Encourage students to proofread their work.
- Computer software that reads a student's work out loud can help identify grammatical errors and spelling mistakes.
- Encouraging a student to proofread their work in stages can also help (for example, focusing first on punctuation, then the use of capitals, then spelling, etc.).

Develop spoken communication

- Keep instructions short.
- Repeat instructions if necessary.
- Allow students to record instruction using an audio recorder such as an mp3 recorder, mini-disc player or dictaphone.

Utilize a multisensory approach

- Adopt a multisensory approach to teaching. Use visual, auditory and kinaesthetic activities.
- Engage taste and smell.

Dysgraphia

Dysgraphia is a difficulty in putting thoughts into writing and generally takes the form of poor handwriting. Sometimes difficulties in organization and fine motor coordination are apparent. Typically a student with dysgraphia will make spelling errors, reverse letters and numbers and have poor or no use of punctuation. Problems with written communication can lead to stress and frustration. It is thought that when apparent in adults it is due to head trauma. A child with dysgraphia will usually have a sibling or family member with the condition.

Strategies to use with students with dysgraphia

- Encourage students to talk out loud as they write. This will provide valuable auditory feedback. Get students to dictate their thoughts onto tape as they work.
- Allow more time for written tasks (e.g. notetaking, exams). It can be tiring for the student to complete the work so allow for regular breaks.
- Utilize support staff and peers to check work for errors.
- Remove neatness or spelling as grading criteria for some assignments.
- Materials – use paper with squares or lines as this will help organization and improve legibility of writing.
- Presentation – encourage the student to redraft their work (e.g. use a double page: the left-hand page for the first draft, the right-hand page for the amended work).
- Electronic resources – make use of a dictaphone or mini-disc player as an auditory diary, or for notemaking. Spellcheckers can help, as can an electronic personal organizer.
- Draft ideas in diagramatic form, for example use spider diagrams, flow charts or idea mapping.
- Motivation and self-esteem – reassure and motivate the student. For example, tell them that lots of famous and successful people have similar difficulties.

Dyscalculia

Dyscalculia is a condition affecting a person's ability to understand, remember and use numbers. A student with dyscalculia will have difficulty visualizing numbers and mathematical processes. Their confidence and self-esteem will be poor. They will also have difficulties with spelling, handwriting and reading especially to do with detail that needs to be memorized. No definitive cause has been found but potential causes include neurological problems and it could be a hereditary condition.

Strategies to use with students who have dyscalculia

- Encourage the student to read the problem out loud – auditory skills may be a strength of the student.
- Visualize mathematical problems (for example, draw pictures).
- Take extra time to look at any visual information that may be provided.

- Spend extra time helping the student to memorize mathematical facts. For example use music, rhyme and repetition.
- Make sure worksheets are uncluttered – so that the student is not overwhelmed by too much visual information.
- Allow extra time for exams: a student with a dyscalculia type difficulty may be allowed extra time to complete tests and may be able to use a calculator for exams, but this will have to be noted on any certificates gained.
- Use graph paper for mathematical work as this will help to keep the numbers in line.

Dyspraxia

This is also known as a developmental coordination disorder. A student with dyspraxia will have some form of motor or sensory impairments resulting in difficulties in coordination. They are also likely to have difficulties in organizing their thoughts, they are frequently late and have trouble concentrating on a task. In large groups listening can be difficult and they lack understanding of non-verbal signals tending to take things literally. Their writing and drawing skills are often poor. Many students with dyspraxia have low self-esteem and get easily stressed, depressed and anxious. They may have difficulty maintaining relationships with peers. Causes are thought to be delayed neurological development or some form of brain damage.

Strategies to use with students who have dyspraxia

Develop motor-coordination activities

- Develop activities to aid coordination skills.

Develop ways to build self-esteem

- Focus on the student's positive points, giving praise where appropriate. However, ensure you praise other students at the same time to avoid claims of unfair treatment.

Utilize external support

- Often support from external agencies such as educational psychologists, speech therapists and physiotherapists can be beneficial.

Encourage appropriate choice of clothing

- Shoes – use velcro shoes to avoid the frustration of tying shoe laces.
- Loose or baggy clothes can help when getting clothes on or off.
- Choose clothes which have a clearly distinguished front and back (e.g. v-neck jumpers).

- More information can be found in O'Regan (2005).

Other strategies that may be useful

- Give clear instructions, ensuring the student is still and has eye contact.
- Use visual cues when giving verbal instructions.
- Do not give too much information at one time.
- Sit the student where there are minimal distractions. Ensure they can see and hear well.
- Break down activities and tasks into small components.
- Being calm, quiet and above all patient will help in dealing with a dyspraxic student.

Other conditions

The conditions listed above could be described as developmental disorders, a term explained in the opening of this chapter. The following conditions are not directly related to developmental disorders and relate to neurological or extreme behavioural disorders.

Tourette's Syndrome (TS)

Tourette's Syndrome is an inherited neurological disorder. The main identifying factor is multiple motor (body) tics or vocal (phonic) tics which are difficult to control and may get both better and worse over time. Some of the common tics experienced by students with TS are eye blinking, head jerking, making obscene gestures and saying obscene words, sniffing, clearing the throat and spitting. A student with TS may have a short temper and show defiant behaviours towards those in authority. They often give the appearance of not listening. TS is often an inherited condition and factors occurring up to five months prior to birth may increase the severity of the tics (e.g. maternal smoking, maternal stress). Brain abnormalities are also thought to be a potential cause.

Strategies to use with students who have Tourette's Syndrome

Develop therapy

- Encourage students to practise a common tic. This can lead to a tic-free period afterwards.

The importance of diet

- Checking the diet of students with TS may help their behaviour. Additives in food can have a negative effect on them. Certain supplements are helpful.

Relaxation strategies

- Symptoms may be alleviated with relaxation or concentration on an absorbing task.

Classroom environment

- Allow the student to sit near the door, so that they can leave the classroom easily if necessary.
- Periods of time out from the classroom should be available if required.

Rewards and sanctions to use with TS students

- Be consistent with rewards and sanctions.
- Discuss sanctions with the student so that they understand why these sanctions are occurring.

Other strategies that may be useful

- Educating family members, teachers and peers about TS can help.
- Do not draw attention to tics.
- Avoid confrontational situations where possible.

Conduct Disorder (CD)

Students with a conduct disorder will usually display repetitive aggressive, disruptive and defiant behavior, which is usually a call for attention and help. Students with CD tend to violate other people's rights through:

- bullying behaviour
- damaging and ruining the property of other students
- persistently threatening other students
- frequently starting fights.

They often lie to obtain goods or favours or to avoid responsibility. These students often run away from home and play truant from school. Potential causes include family issues, friendship problems, cultures which fail to instill discipline and genetics.

Strategies to use with students who have Conduct Disorder

Set behaviour expectations

- The basic drive of a student with CD is to resist control and manipulation from any adult.
- The more controlling an adult appears to be, the more oppositional the student becomes.
- These students need to have a sense of safety and structure.
- They need guidance.
- Teach the student the appropriate behaviour expected in various situations.

Reinforce positive behavior

- Reward the students when they display good behaviour.
- Clear and consistent rewards can break the cycle of negative behaviour and sanctions.

Therapy

- Provide a child with CD the option to talk through their behaviour. Different forms of therapy may be necessary to help a child control different aspects of their behaviour:
  - Family therapy – it could be useful to look at issues of communication, reducing blame and building relationships between family members. This is usually a short term-solution.
  - Cognitive Behaviour Therapy (CBT) – this enables a student to deal with conflict, identify and understand their thoughts and feelings, and thus aids their behaviour in social settings. This form of therapy is useful with older children, displaying mild characteristics of CD.

Pathological Demand Avoidance syndrome (PDA)

This is a pervasive developmental disorder, which is related to but separate from the autistic spectrum. Students with PDA tend to resist and avoid all demands asked of them. They are socially manipulative, avoid everyday rules and expectations, have frequent and rapid moods changes and have a lack of reality. Students with PDA have to be in control of situations and can appear overbearing. They want to do everything on their own terms. They have rapid mood changes and when frustrated can often have violent outbursts. They lack a sense of responsibility and usually underachieve in school often producing only a minimum amount of work. They find it hard to negotiate with other students. It is thought that PDA is caused by some form of brain dysfunction with genetic factors, but more research is needed in this area.

Strategies to use with students who have PDA

Develop ways to keep students on task

- A student with PDA learns best on a one-to-one basis with an adult.

Develop ways to ensure retention of learning

- Allocate a significant proportion of time to monitoring retention of information.
- Repetition is beneficial, thus one-to-one working is again useful.

Develop ways to minimize disruptions

- Not all students with PDA are actively disruptive; however, many students are.
- Often students will behave and comply more in a school setting, then misbehave at home.
- No matter what behaviour a student may use to avoid work, a teacher should remain calm, paying as little attention as possible to the behaviour, and continuing with the work.
- Prevent teasing and bullying from other students as much as possible.

Ways to provide support

- Be tolerant of the student. Being imaginative, determined to succeed and expressing a positive interest in the student are essential to succeed in helping with PDA.
- Give the student 15-minutes counselling time at the start and end of the day. Treat an angry outburst as a panic attack (which it is) and use reassurance rather than blame.

Teaching style

- Be indirect in all demands. For example, use comments like 'I wonder how you do this'.
- Use humour, role play and be flexible and imaginative.
- Introduce goals gradually; give more choice in activities.
- Avoid over-praising the student as this can be detrimental. Some students tear up work which has been praised.
- Avoid negative behaviours as much as possible.

Develop relationships

- Develop strong, trusting relationships.
- Be calm in interactions, avoiding showing frustration, fear or anger at a student.

Use of role play

- Role play and pretending are strengths of a student with PDA so use these to aid their learning. For example allow the student to take the role of the teacher.

Key points

Key points to think about from this chapter are:

- likely reasons for the development of syndromes and conditions
- descriptions of the more common syndromes and conditions
- signs that a student has the syndrome or condition
- strategies to use with learners with the condition.

Motivating students to learn through building good relationships and creating positive learning environments

5

The key to motivating students to learn is to develop good relationships with them based on mutual respect and recognition which helps rapport to be developed. Using positive phrasing can make a significant difference to our relationships with students. Leo Buscaglia (a professor in the department of Special Needs at the University of Southern California) famously said 'fantastic things happen to the way we feel, to the way we make people feel. All this simply by using positive words'. Often disaffected students can 'awfulize' and be very negative about their own ability. They carry a lot of 'psychological junk mail'. By using positive phrasing we can change their attitudes and make them believe that they can achieve. In Chapter 2, we looked in some detail at how we can improve students' self-esteem and self-belief. We can motivate students and create positive learning environments by using rapport-building strategies which will develop good relationships with students. In Chapter 3 we looked at the importance of body language, positioning and vocal matching in building rapport. Vizard (2007a) reinforces the importance of rapport and relationships when he states that there are ten Rs of positive behaviour management:

- recognition
- rapport
- respect
- relationships
- responsibility
- resilience

- rewards
- rules
- rights
- routines.

Relationships are built on respect and understanding. If respect is mutual then often students are less likely to pose behaviour problems and are more willing to engage with the work.

Many students who are disaffected will arrive in class in an agitated state. Often they are in 'survival mode' because the fight/flight reptilian centre of the brain has been stimulated. Often this leads to adrenalin flowing through the body and they feel easily distractable, tense and are unable to settle and concentrate. This adrenalin needs to be used up and activities which involve movement can be useful (for example brain breaks – see Chapter 8).

The type of environment you develop in the classroom and your interactions can start to relax these students. Adopting a relaxed posture and minimizing arm and body shifts can help. Also the tone and speed of vocal delivery can help. By slowing your speech and lowering the volume you can induce a relaxed state. As we shall cover in Chapter 7, an emphasis on fun can release happy hormones (endorphins) and can reduce levels of the stress hormones adrenalin and cortisol in learners.

All of us suffer from recognition hunger – our need for recognition and acknowledgement by others. To build good relationships and to create positive learning environments the following should be developed:

- Meet and greet students as they arrive at the classroom door. Establish eye contact and, with a smile, welcome the students.
- Be interested in them as individuals.
- Use first names.
- When students exit the lesson stand by the door and thank them for their contributions.
- Be open in you body language, avoiding building barrier positions (for example, standing behind a table).
- When settling the group, spot the students who are conforming – thank the group for arriving on time and bringing the right materials. The time to deal with those who do not comply is later, privately, when you move around the room. Thus it is easier to get positive attention than negative attention. This positive approach means that disengaged students are less likely to misbehave and are more likely to conform.
- When speaking to the group ensure that your body language is positive by using:
  - positive gestures
  - smiles
  - appropriate eye contact
  - appropriate body stance
  - facial expressions that are relaxed and positive
  - a positive tone of voice.

- Have a series of positive non-verbal cues that you use.
- When speaking to the class ensure that you use positive phrasing – focus on what they should be doing. Some examples of this could be:
  - Avoid using phrases such as 'don't' as this tends to encourage the behaviour to which you are referring. If we are told in a restaurant not to touch the plate because it is hot we are automatically attracted to touching it to see how hot it is. A burnt finger is usually the result.
  - To enhance a positive sense of community use more rounded words such as 'we' and 'our' rather then 'I', 'my', 'if' and 'but'.
  - Positioning when speaking to students is important. Use proximity and level. Sitting next to a student or kneeling beside them when sanctioning or giving praise keeps their dignity intact. All of us have a personal space bubble around us (a comfort zone) of 50cm so respecting that zone is key.
  - When discussing an issue, standing face-to-face can be unhelpful. Using a psychological geography can be helpful. If you stand alongside someone or at right angles to them you are more likely to have a successful outcome.
  - Peripheral praise also works when you need to get a student to reflect on their behaviour. Praise students either side of the student. For example:
      Student to left – 'Thank you (name) for arriving on time.'
      Student to right – 'Thanks for bringing all the material required.'
      Student in middle – Give a quick sideways glance towards
      them, saying nothing and then move away.
      Using peripheral praise can have a powerful impact on the student to whom you say nothing.
- Give out nuggets of praise when they do something noteworthy – it is essential to 'catch 'em being good'.
- Give written praise which is personalized.
- Respect their opinion.
- When they are speaking maintain appropriate eye contact.
- Use silence when students have spoken to show that you are reflecting on what they have said before responding.

Remember it is your response that will have a significant influence on your students. Teachers' responses to a situation can

> serve as mirrors through which children see and judge their image. If a positive image is reflected, children will feel worthy of love and valued. On the contrary, if the image is negative, children will believe that they are rejected, unloved and unwanted and they will act accordingly (de Andres 1999, p. 88).

So it is essential that we are careful in how we respond verbally and non-verbally to students.

Rewards

Students of all ages appreciate rewards. They do not like rewards when they are unwarranted and sometimes when they are given publicly. Rewards can take the form of verbal and written praise and a range of non-verbal cues including smiles and gestures such as thumbs-up. The best tangible reward systems are those developed with students. They can help select which rewards would hold currency with them. They can help in the design of reward postcards and stickers. Some rewards that work well are:

- stickers
- praise postcards – designed as 'Top Trump' collector cards
- privileges for students who achieve a certain level
- golden time – minutes collected for good work where students are given time to do something they like at the end of the session
- discount cards to local shops related to rewards
- prize draws made with raffle tickets given out for positive behaviour or good work
- pin badges relating to subject areas
- rewards for attendance and punctuality
- colour discs are placed in a jar with the students' names on them and they are counted at the end of the week; rewards are given in relation to the number collected
- teaching and learning money which is given out when the skill of the week is acquired
- rewards linked to leisure centre facilities
- group rewards, for example, marbles are put into a jar and the level of the reward is based on the number of marbles collected.

Case Study

In one school for students with social, emotional and behavioural difficulties in the south-west of England, a teacher discusses at the beginning of the week the behavioural targets for any student who is experiencing difficulties in managing aspects of their behaviour.

With the student's permission the member of staff shares these targets with the rest of the group. The group decides what reward as a group they would like to receive if the student achieves these targets. During the week the group actively encourages the student to achieve these targets. This has proven to be a very successful behaviour modification strategy which is linked to a reward system.

Learning environments

How we arrange furniture, resources and displays can have a significant impact on students and their learning. Jensen (2003) reinforces this when he states: 'Avoid being passive about the environment: It does matter . . . Take charge: do your best to support your students in being their very best by orchestrating powerful learning environments.' It is essential that we create vibrant and colourful learning environments. A large proportion of learning takes place peripherally and most of this impact is at a subconscious level. This section will look at key points to consider in developing a positive learning environment.

Peripheral learning

Below are some examples of peripheral learning notices.

> • I can't do it – YET.
>
> • Are you talking to yourself enough (good learners do it more).
>
> • Mistakes are my friends – they help me learn.
>
> • We're not here to work ...we're here to learn.
>
> • The person who has never made a mistake never tried anything new – Albert Einstein.
>
> • Never, never, never give up – Winston Churchill.
>
> • Personally I'm always ready to learn, although I do not always like being taught – Winston Churchill.
>
> • Too hot, too cold, too still, too thirsty, too hungry and you can't learn much.
>
> • Take time to think.
>
> • You never know how much you can do until you try.

Below are examples of positive peripheral learning notices that you can use in the classroom. They clearly thank students in advance for the expected behaviour:

- Thank you for bringing all the materials and equipment needed for the lesson.
- Thank you for helping.
- Thank you for wearing your full school uniform.
- Thank you for thinking of others.
- Thank you for listening when others are talking.
- Thank you for thinking before you speak.
- Thank you for being polite.
- Thank you for always respecting other people.
- Thank you for putting up your hand to answer a question.

Lighting

Use of fluorescent lights can have a negative effect and cause learners to misbehave. The imperceptible flicker they create can impair concentration. Reflected light from interactive whiteboards can have a negative effect on students' vision and can cause eye fatigue. If light levels are too low serotonin production is reduced and can cause depression. We need to generate about 2,500 lux in a classroom. Outdoor lighting is typically 10,000 lux. Dim lighting, when using film or DVD in the classroom, will only provide 10–20 lux and can lead to sleepiness. Keep lighting bright but not too bright.

Temperature

Keep temperature reasonably low in classrooms. If the temperature increases above 22C then problems can arise. High temperatures increase neurotransmitter levels which can cause increased aggressiveness. Classroom temperatures between 20C and 22C are best. Keep the air circulating as stagnant air is unhealthy.

Ionization

With all the electrical equipment used today, the air is full of positive ions whose electrical charges can make us feel groggy, sleepy and depressed. It is important to reduce the level of positive ions by turning off equipment when not in use and by getting a de-ionizer.

Colour

Too much visual clutter and bright colours can cause students with some syndromes and conditions to become distressed and display poor behaviour. Pastel shades should be used on classroom walls. It has a calming effect, can create positive emotions and improve concentration.

Plants

These can remove CO_2 and increase oxygen levels in learning environments. This is increasingly necessary with new school designs, which are built to be energy efficient to reduce heat loss. This results in higher CO_2 levels which displace oxygen. Students can become sleepy and find their ability to learn is reduced. Plants can also improve productivity. Getting disengaged students to nurture and care for these plants can have a positive effect on them.

Research Zone

Reading University and University College of London (2008) ran tests in eight primary schools and found that new-build schools (as part of the government's Building Schools for the Future initiative) are designed to be more airtight to save energy and reduce heat loss. As a result these buildings have high CO_2 levels which once breathed in gets into the blood and into the brain. This lack of oxygen causes students to become drowsy, their reaction times were slower and memory was affected. Their ability to absorb new information was reduced.

Rehydration points

Encouraging students to rehydrate by having water dispensers in the room can be useful. The brain uses 30 per cent of the water consumed by our bodies. Water is the basis of electrical firings in the brain. We need 1–1.5 litres a day, which can be found in fruit, vegetables and other food items as well as directly from water.

Furniture and its arrangement

Furniture design is important for comfort and to aid good posture. Adjustable sloping table tops are important with steps for students to support their feet. The arrangement of the tables is important; pairing seats and putting them in rows can improve behaviour.

Hughes and Vass (2001, p. 88) quote a modern foreign languages teacher who obviously understands the importance of the environment. 'When they walk into my room they'll walk into France. They'll see hear smell and "feel" France. They'll speak French, they'll feel French and they'll almost be French.'

 Top Tip

Positive learning environments

These are key things to consider when developing Positive Learning Environments according to teachers in a number of institutions in the north-west of England. They show how you can develop Positive Learning Environments verbally, non-verbally, through use of rewards and by taking into account key considerations in the physical environment.

Verbally	Non-verbally
<ul><li>positive reinforcement – praise</li><li>set ground rules with student input</li><li>humour</li><li>have a self-effacing quality</li><li>talking to them as equals</li><li>clear instructions</li><li>respectful</li><li>tone varied for praise and discipline</li><li>calm/soft voice</li><li>develop positive communication</li><li>use student names</li><li>be fair and considerate</li><li>thanks</li><li>personal praise</li><li>highlight exemplar students</li><li>repeating what a student says to demonstrate active listening</li><li>good communication – clear, concise and at an appropriate level</li><li>welcome students – friendly rapport, positive greetings at the beginning and farewell at the end</li><li>well done</li><li>congratulations</li><li>be supportive – reassuring, mistakes are OK</li><li>be assertive</li><li>appropriate differentiation</li><li>pace of session – keep it moving quickly – chunk down work</li></ul>	<ul><li>show respect, have positive regard</li><li>smiling</li><li>friendly expressions</li><li>positive hand gestures</li><li>nodding and supportive listening</li><li>positive eye contact</li><li>focus on them as individuals</li><li>getting onto their level</li><li>sit down with them, crouching by their side</li><li>structured lessons</li><li>body position/posture</li><li>positive body language and non-verbal cues</li><li>open stance</li><li>presence</li><li>respect</li><li>being there for them</li><li>thumbs-up</li><li>recognition</li><li>mood of tutor – busy syndrome</li><li>being prepared – enough work</li><li>punctual – timely</li><li>clear resources – interactive, inclusive, interesting</li><li>theatrics – it is a performance</li><li>written reinforcers on work</li></ul>
Physical	**Rewards**
<ul><li>displays<ul><li>peripheral learning notices</li><li>aspirational notices</li><li>displays of students' work selected by students to show their own learner profile</li><li>graffiti board</li><li>information on learning and the brain in poster form</li><li>colourful</li></ul></li><li>notices<ul><li>made by learners</li><li>stimulating, relevant to topic</li><li>promoting positive behaviour</li></ul></li><li>room layout varied</li><li>tidy room – clean tidy bright environment</li><li>planned seating</li><li>regular changes to seating</li><li>clear instructions</li><li>adequate resources</li><li>visual aids</li><li>classroom temperature/ventilation, heat, fresh air</li></ul>	<ul><li>praise postcards sent home</li><li>collectibles – Top Trump type cards but at three levels: gold, silver, bronze</li><li>pin badges</li><li>showing good examples of work to rest of class</li><li>student of the month</li><li>trips/visits</li><li>stickers</li><li>praise</li><li>sweets</li><li>recognition</li><li>serious prizes – periodic regular prizes</li><li>public acknowledgement</li><li>fun</li><li>peer praise</li><li>Oscar ceremony</li><li>group rewards</li></ul> $\Rightarrow$

- varied groups of students
- smell – aromatherapy – zingy, citrusy
- lighting as appropriate
- background music – appropriate to group or topic
- comfortable surroundings
- welcome door mat
- room open for learning shop sign on door
- safe
- comfort breaks
- no outside distractions
- no low-level disruptions
- consider Maslow's hierarchy of needs
- positive messages in classroom and in the corridor

By building good relationships through a positive, supportive and caring attitude in a learning environment which we have made positive I believe that disaffected students will feel safe and secure and will thrive.

Key points

Key points to think about from this chapter are:

- the ten Rs of positive behaviour management
- how to build good relationships and create a positive learning environment
- the types of rewards that can be given to students
- the elements of the learning environment that should be developed.

Personalizing learning through developing individual learner profiles

6

With all students it is important to ensure that learning is personalized and that their experiences in learning relate specifically to their needs. They should be treated as partners in their learning. With disaffected students it is essential that we understand what makes up their individual learner profile and be responsive to the ways that these students can achieve the best. This is reinforced by Best and Thomas (2007, p. 146): 'Personalized learning equates to learning that respects individual needs, aptitude, learning preferences and interests of learners – with the key aim of ensuring that every learner achieves the highest standards possible.' To achieve this we need to:

- have learning conversations with our students
- use open questioning with them to help them be more reflective
- listen to learners – encourage the student voice with individual groups; use this to personalize learning and drive improvement
- encourage learners to identify their preferred learning styles
- empower learners to take responsibility for their own learning to help to develop the neo-cortex area of the brain which when mature helps with planning, organization and more mature behaviour – encourage them to have a sense of ownership and control over their learning
- develop their capacity to study independently
- identify learner strengths and weaknesses through assessment
- ensure that gifted and talented students are stretched and that there is appropriate support for those students with additional or special needs
- develop social communication skills and personal management that learners will need
- develop collaborative learning environments where cooperative learning is a regular feature (refer to Chapter 8 for more details on cooperative learning)
- have high quality teaching and learning take place
- develop powerful learning environments where resources are well organized and peripheral learning can take place (refer to Chapter 5)
- use variable pupil groupings

- target set, track and monitor students' progress
- use personal tutors, learning guides and mentors to support students in their learning journey and to be proactive by being the point of contact for the student's family. The government, in 'The Children's Plan' (2007), stated that they aim to introduce learning guides for each pupil to help them work to their full potential by 2010 – they also want personal tutors who know the students well to act as a main contact for parents
- develop family learning weeks to help develop a learning partnership
- develop reflective logs or learning journals for students
- intervene quickly when students' performance and work dip
- develop cross-agency working to support students, particularly those facing difficulties
- look at how to extend the curriculum using outside organizations and local environment.

The 'Report of the Teaching and Learning in 2020' Review Group (2008) summarized personalized learning well:

> Put simply, personalised learning and teaching means taking a highly structured and responsive approach to each child's and young person's learning, in order that all are able to progress, achieve and participate. It means strengthening the link between learning and teaching by engaging pupils – and their parents – as partners in learning.

In order to personalize our teaching we need to be able to differentiate the work so that each student is able to engage and have successful learning experiences. For this to occur students need to explore their unique learner profile. Some of the key areas to consider are given below.

Learning style analysis

Prashnig (2006) in her book *Learning Styles in Action* has developed a very comprehensive and different approach to analysing learning styles in students. Her 'learning style analysis' looks at the following areas:

- left/right hemispheric dominance – related to information processing and thinking styles
- sensory preferences – visual, auditory, kinaesthetic (further information on this can be found in the Top Tips in Chapter 1)
- physical domain – importance of food and drink; time of day that is best to study and levels of mobility needed when learning (for example – stationary or moving around)
- environmental factors – light, temperature, sound, work zone (refer to Chapter 5)
- social dimension – team or individual player, working in groups (refer to Chapter 8)
- attitudes – motivation, persistence, structure and responsibility.

Each student reflects on these areas and a profile summary is produced of student preferences and how they learn best. The non-preferences of learners are also listed.

Both lists can be used as a starting point for personal tutors and learning guides in their learning conversations with students. When developing learners, staff should try to get students to develop areas indicated as non-preferences, to develop a fuller range of approaches to learning. The learning style analysis survey also provides group data which can be used to target different approaches in our teaching which takes into account the full range of learner profiles in a particular group. Her work is based on the work of Dunn and Dunn (1998) on learning and working styles. More information can be found at her website (www.creativelearningcentre.com).

Case Study

One large Pupil Referral Unit (PRU) in central England has used the work of Barbara Prashnig and the Creative Learning Company to produce profiles of learning and working styles of individual students. The online analysis builds up a clear picture of student preferences relating to learning and working styles. They use student non-preference profiling to develop learning strengths.

This approach has been very successful in engaging students who are very disaffected and have had little success in school environments.

Sensory preferences

In Chapter 1 (Top Tip section) we looked at how we might detect the sensory preference of a student by looking at eye movements and by listening to the words a student uses. There are a number of questionnaires available to identify sensory preferences. For example Smith's (1996) work on accelerated learning (see further Smith 1996, pp. 44–5).

The main sensory preferences are:

- visual
- auditory
- kinaesthetic – movement
- olfactory – smell
- gustatory – taste.

Sensory preferences are our preferred way of taking in our world and experiences. Twenty per cent of learners have such a strong sensory preference that they can only take in information if it is presented in that style. We tend to teach in our own sensory preference but it is important that we teach using a range of sensory preferences. So try to include some of each of the following:

- Using visual sensory predicates: for example, 'I see what you mean'; 'picture that'; 'looking closely'; and use lots of images (photos, diagrams, posters, PowerPoint, graphics, keywords displayed around the room).
- Using auditory sensory predicates: for example, 'I hear what you are saying'; 'That sounds good'; 'I'm speechless'; and use presentations involving teacher talk; encourage students to describe learning to each other; use music in lessons; group discussions; readings; debates; rhymes.
- Using kinaesthetic sensory predicates: for example, 'Let's talk about it'; 'hit the nail on the head'; and use role play, modelling, physical activities including brain breaks, design and build and lots of non-verbal communication (tics and tells).

Multiple intelligences

Gardner developed a model of intelligences which were groupings of abilities or skills which students use in processing information. Each student will have a balance of these. It is important to develop a range of intelligences in individual learners to help them tackle work. Tests have been developed to help students to identify their prominent intelligences.

- interpersonal
- intrapersonal
- linguistic
- mathematical and logical
- visual and spatial
- kinaesthetic
- musical.

Based on these areas we can attribute key learning tips to each intelligence. Once learners have learnt their dominant intelligence they can use the following key attributes of each and the learning tips to help them in their work. The learning tips are particularly useful in helping engage disaffected students.

Interpersonal intelligence

A student whose dominant intelligence is interpersonal intelligence will be able to:

- see things from many perspectives
- communicate well both verbally and non-verbally
- be comfortable forming, building and maintaining relationships socially with others
- work in teams and make a significant contribution.

> **Learning Tips**
>
> **Students could revise in a social setting – maybe have a group of friends together for a revision weekend.**
>
> **Students could work in pairs, each learning different facts from a topic. They could then teach the other student what they have learnt.**

Intrapersonal skills

Students whose dominant intelligence is intrapersonal intelligence will:

- be self-motivated
- use journals and diaries for their work
- try to find explanations for their thoughts feelings and emotions
- take time to be quiet and reflect.

> **Learning Tips**
>
> **Students could set themselves targets.**
>
> **Students could talk to themselves about what they are trying to learn.**

Linguistic intelligence

A student who has a well-developed linguistic intelligence will:

- be a good listener and also communicate well in both written and spoken modes
- learn through listening, writing, reading and discussion
- copy linguistic idiosyncrasies of others
- use the written or spoken word to amuse, entertain and convey information.

> **Learning Tips**
>
> **Students could learn using rhymes, mnemonics, raps.**
>
> **Students could use flashcards which have words on one side and explanations on the other.**

Mathematical and logical intelligence

Students with mathematical and logical intelligence will:

- be good at solving logical puzzles
- spot patterns in relationships
- understand at an early stage the concepts of time, space, quantity, number and cause and effect
- be capable of mathematical thinking, for example, make hypotheses, gather evidence, estimate and build models.

> **Learning Tips**
>
> **Students could use memory maps, spider diagrams and lists.**
>
> **Students could also write everything they need to know about a topic on one sheet of paper.**

Visual and spatial intelligence

Students with visual and spatial intelligence will:

- learn through seeing and observing and make use of memory maps
- be good at visualizing and imagining scenes
- have an understanding of graphs, maps and other visual representations
- be able to construct three dimensional objects and imagine how they are constructed.

> **Learning Tips**
>
> **Students could use memory maps to help them remember facts.**
>
> **Students could attach pictures to key words they need to remember.**

Kinaesthetic intelligence

A student who has a well-developed kinaesthetic intelligence will:

- learn through doing
- learn through touch, movement, manipulation and physical experience
- enjoy activities such as field trips, model building, role play and video productions
- often be restless.

Musical intelligence

A student with musical intelligence will show some ability to:

- enjoy improvising and playing with different sorts of sounds
- have a good sense of rhythm and be able to respond to music by dance, drama or composing
- be sensitive to mood changes in sounds and be able to pick out sounds of individual instruments
- show an interest in and have the ability to play a musical instrument.

 Top Tip

In helping learners to be successful with their work and in revision, encourage them to use the learning tips associated with their dominant multiple intelligences.

Hemispheric dominance

The brain is made up of a number of different areas which have specific functions. The neo-cortex found at the top of the brain (looking rather like the cap on a field mushroom) is divided into two parts, the left and right side. These two sides are connected by a cord known as the corpus callosum. In males this connecting cord makes 30 per cent fewer connections due to the effect of oestrogen and testosterone surges while the foetus is developing. This affects only male foetuses and leads to a slight delay in left-side development of the brain when the corpus callosum is trying to connect the left side of the brain to the right side. The more left- and right-brain activities you use in class, particularly by using the senses, the more connections your students will make, the more they will remember and the faster they will think. When we use only one half of the brain it learns at 35 per cent efficiency, but when both halves are used it means that we learn at over 80 per cent efficiency. Brain break activities are particularly good at linking both hemispheres of the brain (refer to Chapter 8). The left side of the brain (logic hemisphere) is the part of the brain that is most useful for students in school. The right side (gestalt hemisphere) is the creative side. Typical features of each are:

Left side

- sequential
- linear
- logical
- detail important
- works from parts to whole.

Right side

- random
- intuitive
- spontaneous
- curious
- works from whole to part.

 Top Tip

Encourage students to use both sides of the brain, for example, encourage right-handed people to use their left hand for some tasks and left-handed people to use their right hand for some tasks. Another activity might be to get students who normally use their right foot to practise ball skills with their left foot or vice versa.

This chapter has outlined a variety of strategies we can use with students to help them identify and understand their individual learner profiles. It gives ideas for personalizing the learning experience to ensure all learners can achieve the highest standard possible.

Key points

Key points to think about from this chapter are:

- what is personalized learning and how to develop an individual learner profile
- learning style analysis
- sensory preferences
- multiple intelligences
- hemispheric dominance.

7

Focus on fun: Making lessons enjoyable and entertaining

Why give this chapter the title 'Focus on fun'? Well, researchers have found that laughter can have a most positive effect on learning; laughing lessons really are good for learning. Jensen (2004, p. 65) tells us that: 'Laughter increases the flow of neurotransmitters that are required for alertness and memory . . . Laughter provides a break in routine and relaxes students who may be stressed or anxious.'

Many disaffected students are stressed and anxious. Gilbert (2006) quoting Andrew Curran (a consultant paediatric neurologist) suggests that learners can feel low, angry, reactive and switched off because they have constantly been told they are no good in their work. This disengages the brain and leaves them with a strong sense of feeling incapable and stupid: 'If your heart's not engaged then your head don't work' (Curran cited in Gilbert 2006, p. 6). Smith (2002, pp. 117–18) states that: 'Laughter in the classroom can be a very positive way to reduce stress and aid learning . . . We become more able to deal with cognitive challenge when we approach the challenge having shared laughter with others.'

Smith goes on to suggest that laughter also:

- lowers resting blood pressure
- reduces stress
- enhances the immune system
- reduces the symptoms of depression
- improves sleep.

Fry, a Stanford University psychiatrist quoted in Burgess (2000, p. 2) says that 'Laughter is an excellent workout for the body'. The positive effects he mentions are listed below:

- stimulates circulation
- exercises the lungs

- benefits the heart and respiratory system
- raises endorphin levels.

Blood pressure actually increases when laughing but then drops below a normal resting level after you have stopped laughing. Laughter leads to a decrease in levels of the stress hormone cortisol in the system. The classroom is a good place for humour as people are 30 times more likely to laugh in social settings. Research has shown that children laugh more than adults: they laugh 300 times a day compared with 50 times for adults. We need to engage with learners more through humour. When we laugh our brain releases chemicals called endorphins. These are relaxants and create feelings of happiness. Dopamine is another feel good hormone that is released when you expect or get a reward. Imagine looking at your favourite box of chocolates and waiting a moment before selecting a flavour. Plenty of dopamine will be surging through your veins at this point. Gilbert (2006) citing Curran writes that dopamine is the best memory-boosting neurochemical, stating the importance of encouraging teachers to implement fun and creative classroom practices to bring about the release of these positive chemicals.

Endorphins are also released when we exercise, hence the importance of brain breaks in lessons (see Chapter 8). Laughter leads to better problem-solving. It is important to incorporate fun activities in our teaching practices in order to enable the release of these chemicals, which can bring about a more positive learning environment for students.

Gilbert (2006, p. 6) says that a fun learning environment is essential for disengaged students, allowing them to 'rediscover their childlike curiosity for learning and to begin the rebuilding of their confidence and expectation of themselves'.

Burgess (2000, p. 2) suggests that when students are engaged and interested then achievement follows. 'The brain is designed to scan for novelty. Thus by creating a happy, interesting, stimulating and laughing classroom we help to promote better learning.'

Novelty

To get students' attention we need to introduce novelty into the lesson and to develop sudden changes. The novelty centre of the brain starts to be fully active in adolescence. Some useful techniques may include:

- Using props, puppets and costumes to grab their attention.
- Using teasers where you get students to do an activity such as rotating the right foot in a clockwise direction and then getting the right hand to draw a figure of six (see Chapter 8 p. 81 for this and more ideas). Get them to think about why their foot changes direction when their hand draws a figure six during the lesson – giving the answer at the end.

- Using cliffhangers at the end of the lesson. Give part of a fact related to the next lesson; do not complete it – this is rather like the device used in television soaps such as *Eastenders* or *Coronation Street*.
- Using positive attention getters as a learning ritual. When getting the group back together when a task is completed, give learners a one-minute signal and another one when time is up. Some of the following items could be used:
    - whistle (samba band, clanger type or train whistle)
    - bell (bicycle, counter bell)
    - horn (metal bike horn)
    - animal effects (croaking frog, cricket, elephant).
- Keep attention by using suspense and other inputs such as tragedy and horror.
- Use funny anecdotes – particularly if they relate to you and are self-effacing.
- Use audio clips and DVD inputs which are humorous.
- Introduce 'I say, I say' humour breaks – students form into groups and share appropriate jokes which are not offensive. The group then present their best joke to the other groups.

Case Study

In one Pupil Referral Unit (PRU) in the East Midlands, the headteacher has organized the playground in such a way that an area is given over to Victorian playground games. All students including secondary-aged students are encouraged to be involved in these games at break times. Many staff including the headteacher join in. The playground was an area where a number of conflicts arose. Now it is a positive environment where students can have fun.

Peripheral learning

Peripheral learning can be useful when creating humour in the classroom. For example, notices and slogans such as the ones below can be used to create humour.

- 'It takes 135 muscles to frown and 47 to smile . . . so don't waste energy.'
- 'It takes an estimated 20,000 frowns to make a permanent wrinkle.'
- 'Even if there is nothing to laugh about, laugh on credit.' (Author unknown)
- 'Laughter is a tranquillizer with no side effects.' (Arnold Glasgow)
- 'Humour is a great thing, the saving thing. The minute it crops up, all our irritations and resentments slip away, and a sunny spirit takes their place.' (Mark Twain).

Burgess (2000) in his book on laughing lessons suggests some very interesting ideas on how to create novel and humorous environments. The following items suggested by Burgess, and teachers I have worked with, can be used to create these fun environments:

- shop open/closed sign for door: 'We're open for learning' *or* 'Knowledge given away here – free'
- welcome doormat at entrance
- use unusual signs and display boards from shops and restaurants
- have unusual lights such as lava lamps
- have amusing signs for lockers such as:
  - 'Three-room apartment for rent'
  - 'Keep out'
  - 'Enter at your own risk'
- post amusing sayings and cartoons around the room
- use comics or wrapping paper to back noticeboards.

Other suggestions for ways to keep the environment positive and humorous are:

- inflatables such as dolphins and sharks suspended from the ceiling
- mobiles – space ships – with key words on them
- have a joke board where learners can write jokes
- develop a quotations board where you can display some unusual headlines, or funny signs that have been used, or a range of funny things that have been written or said by students (keeping their anonymity). Some examples are given below:
  - **Headlines**:
    - Stolen painting found by tree
    - Goldfish is saved from drowning
    - I want the Monday edition of the *Sunday Telegraph*
  - **Signs**:
    - Toilet out of order, please use floor below
    - Sign in a London department store: Bargain basement upstairs
    - Sign in an office: After tea break staff should empty the teapot and stand upside down on the draining board
    - Sign on a repair shop door: We can repair anything (please knock hard on the door – the bell doesn't work)
  - **Students' incidental humour**:
    History
    - Joan of Arc was famous as Noah's wife
    - The Trojan War raged between the Greeks and the Tories
    Geography
    - A consonant is a large piece of land surrounded by water
    Science
    - Question: What happens to your body as you age?
      Answer: When you get old, so do your bowels and you get intercontinental.

Activities to keep lessons fun

- Have a box full of props – containing items such as hats, wigs, costumes, oversized hands, glasses and puppets to use when energy levels are flagging.

- Use body-part props – give students happy face masks, quizzical expressions masks, prop arms etc. to use in lessons.
- Have a display tabletop where you can display novel and unusual items.
- Use feely bags to feel objects related to the lesson and get them to identify the object by touch alone.
- Treasure trove – prepare a box with objects in it relating to the lesson theme. For example, in German you could put in the following items for the theme holiday:
  - postcards of a German resort
  - German resort brochures
  - hotel leaflet
  - model aeroplane
  - luggage label.

  The box is passed around and students take an object each and try to identify the theme.
- An extension of the activity above is a card pack which could be given out containing German words all on a theme. Another pack could be given out with the English words to match the German words. Get the students to identify the theme from the German words. Then get them to match the English words to them.

  For example, German words: *das Hotel, der Sommer, der Winter, die Sonne, der Sommerurlaub, der Urlaub, der Winterurlaub.*

  English words: the summer, the winter holiday, the sun, the holiday, the summer, the hotel, the summer holiday.
- Laughter warm-ups – Funes (2000), in her book *Laughing Matters*, talks about the importance of laughter. Based on her laughter work-out activities, we could get students to take part in laughter warm-ups – discovering how many different styles of laughter we have.
  - Facial and vocal cord warm-up:
    - humming deep in your stomach: 'mmmmmm'
    - then add vowels
      'mmmaaamamamama'
      'mmmeeememememe'
      and so on.
    - Then on one breath do the following:
      'hoo hoo hoo/haw haw haw/hee hee hee/hum hum hum'.
    - Try some of the following tongue twisters – try each one just using one breath:
      'If a noisy noise annoys an onion,
      An annoying noisy noise annoys an onion more.'
      'She sells sea shells by the sea shore.
      The shells she sells are surely seashells.
      So if she sells shells on the seashore,
      I'm sure she sells seashore shells'.
    - Then get students into pairs and get them to find their laughter words – all of us have words we find funny and are a trigger for laughter.
- Humour breaks – Jenson (1995) suggests that these are useful to use. For example, all students stand up and close their eyes. If they can think of a joke they raise their hand and keep it up. The whole group opens their eyes and if their hand is not up they cluster around someone who has their hand up. That person tells their joke and their cluster group applauds.
- Use magic tricks with learners – there are many good value sets on the market. This will introduce a lot

of fun to the lesson. Get students to prepare tricks to present to the rest of the class. Some good ones can be found at www.mathsisfun.com.

- Edible maths – use sweets or fruit items to help students with addition, subtraction, multiplication and division. Students eat the answer. For example, 5 – 2 = 3. Three sweets are eaten.
- Exaggerate exaggerate – get students into groups of five and give one student in each group a fact. Their job is to repeat the fact and in turn each group member tries to exaggerate some aspect of the fact – so that by the fifth person the fact is unrecognizable.
- Give out teaching and learning money to learners who manage to develop a key skill, answer a difficult question or use humour appropriately. These notes can then be used to trade in at the stationery shop for items or can be used for privileges.
- Using a range of board games and computer versions of television quiz shows can help increase the fun quotient in the classroom.
- Poker headbands – this activity is based on an idea from Cavert and Frank (1999). A pack of playing cards are shuffled and the teacher places a card in a headband (the number of headbands depends on number of students), without the student seeing their own card. Students are then told that they need to treat each other by the value of the cards they are seeing. The king has the most value and the ace is lowest in value. Students have to try to associate with the high-value cards and stay away from the low-value cards. No student should disclose the value of other students' cards. They need to think about conversation topics to discuss. At the end of the activity get the group into a line and ask them to stand in order of value of cards they think they have – kings at one end and aces at the other. Then get the students to look at their cards and discuss how they felt. You can get students to wear cards that relate to famous characters in history, inventors in science, characters for fiction/plays or objects.
- 'In the words of . . .' – make up a set of cards with key historical dates on them. Students, in groups of five, select a card. Whichever card they choose they have to talk about issues of that date and in the accent, voice or language of that time. For example, 1066 – talk about the impending Norman Conquest.

The range of classroom activities given above which 'focus on fun' will help you manage and engage disaffected students. When facing difficulties we should always remember the importance of humour.

Key points

Key points to think about from this chapter are:

- that focusing on fun in the classroom engages students, reduces stress, lowers blood pressure
- how to generate novelty in the classroom
- how to generate positive and fun peripheral learning notices
- how to do laughter warm-ups
- activities to keep lessons fun.

Making effective use of starter activities, brain breaks and cooperative learning strategies

8

Starter activities

Learners who are disaffected and find it difficult to engage with learning are often extremely kinaesthetic, cannot sit still and have poor concentration. This is also the case for learners with certain syndromes and conditions as described in Chapter 4. These learners also like structure to their lessons and appreciate firm boundaries. It is useful to establish a routine where there is a period of take-up time at the beginning of the lesson in which students are given three minutes to settle and get out any necessary equipment and materials. During this time it is useful to have a starter activity running to focus their attention and to enable them to tune into the lesson. This starter activity could link and act as a bridge with the last lesson or help prepare for the current lesson. It could also be a starter that focuses on a visual, auditory or kinaesthetic approach to engage learners who will have a range of sensory preferences.

A number of ideas for starter activities, are shown over the next few pages.

Alphabet gym (bridge with last lesson)

- Have the alphabet written around the room with the letters L, R or T under each letter.
- This can be done on cards or on an electronic whiteboard.
- Get the students to identify key words from the last lesson, from quite short words to longer words.
- Then in turn go through the list of words.
- Students then have to look at the chart and move their arms and/or legs according to the letter next to the alphabet letter.
  L = left hand and leg
  R = right hand and leg
  T = place left or right hand and/or legs together

For example, CARBON DIOXIDE would be RLLTTR TTTTTTT.

A	B	C	D	E	F	G
L	T	R	T	T	L	R
H	I	J	K	L	M	N
R	T	L	R	L	L	R
O	P	Q	R	S	T	U
T	R	T	L	R	R	L
V	W	X	Y	Z		
T	L	T	R	L		

- You may like to do the same but instead of moving arms and legs use the list below and hop, clap and jump.

a	b	c	d	e	f	g
clap	clap	jump	hop	clap	hop	hop
h	i	j	k	l	m	n
hop	hop	clap	clap	jump	hop	clap
o	p	q	r	s	t	u
jump	clap	hop	hop	clap	jump	jump
v	w	x	y	z		
hop	jump	clap	hop	jump		

All in a spin (group bonding)

- Get the group to sit on chairs in a circle with one less chair than size of group.
- A group member stands in the centre and says 'I am (states their own name) and this is (pointing to and naming another group member)'.
- The person standing in the middle then swaps places with that person, who in turn names another person and swaps places with them until the whole group has taken a turn in the centre.

Alphabet soup

- Prepare a set of laminated alphabet letters (you will need a number of sets to account for words with repeated letters).

- Place an anagram of the lesson's key word on the board. Do this by using Blu Tack on the back of the laminated letters.
- Ask a student to volunteer to rearrange the letters into the key word.

Whole-class bingo

- This activity is a good starter activity, which will help learners to tune in and develop listening skills.
- Below are two versions of bingo:
  1. Using masking tape and A4 sheets of card on which there are key words, make giant bingo boards on the floor (with eight words on each board; two words must be different on each board).
     - Put students into three teams of eight.
     - Read from a script which covers key words or key facts.
     - When a word or fact is mentioned, students cover them by standing on the word or fact.
  2. You could prepare separate small bingo cards for students on A5-sized paper and again read through a script and students cross off words as they are mentioned.
     The winners are the first group or student to cover or cross off all the words on their board.

Change around

- Rearrange the words in each row in the left-hand box (see below) to make a new word in the right-hand box.
- You will notice the old and new words consist of five letters (i.e. DREAD).
- Use the clues to help you.
- In the new-word column, the middle column (third-letter box) for each row is shaded. Once you have found all the new words, the letters in the shaded box will spell out a key word. A clue to the key word can be provided at the beginning of the table.

Example 1: 'Someone who is usually played by men in pantomimes'

Old Words					Clue	New Words				
D	R	E	A	D	Poisonous snake					
T	A	C	K	S	Store one on top of the other					
M	A	T	E	S	Makes domesticated					
T	E	A	M	S	You get this when a kettle boils					
R	O	L	E	S	Not a winner					

Solution:

Old Words					Clue	New Words				
D	R	E	A	D	Poisonous snake	A	D	D	E	R
T	A	C	K	S	Store one on top of the other	S	T	A	C	K
M	A	T	E	S	Makes domesticated	T	A	M	E	S
T	E	A	M	S	You get this when a kettle boils	S	T	E	A	M
R	O	L	E	S	Not a winner	L	O	S	E	R

Key word: DAMES

Example 2: 'You need these if you want to sit down'

Old Words					Clue	New Words				
S	T	O	P	S	These are needed for street lighting					
T	H	E	S	E	You can find this on a bed					
S	T	E	A	L	The smallest					
S	T	A	G	E	Shut this to keep the animals enclosed					
S	H	O	E	S	Firemen use these to put out fires					

Solution:

Old Words					Clue	New Words				
S	T	O	P	S	These are needed for street lighting	P	O	S	T	S
T	H	E	S	E	You can find this on a bed	S	H	E	E	T
S	T	E	A	L	The smallest	L	E	A	S	T
S	T	A	G	E	Shut this to keep the animals enclosed	G	A	T	E	S
S	H	O	E	S	Firemen use these to put out fires	H	O	S	E	S

Key word = SEATS

Clever routes

- Use pages from old road atlases for this activity.
- Students split into pairs and each pair in the whole group is given the same page from an old road atlas.
- Get the whole group to search for specified features on a page which you have given them. For example: town, village, motorway, woodland, church, park.
- The first person in a pair to spot the location gains a point.
- The first student in the group to get ten points wins.

Coded messages

- Can you break the code to reveal the first few lines from a well-known nursery rhyme?
- Not all the letters in the grid (see below) are used in the nursery rhyme.
- For example:
- Wnpx naq Wvyy jrag hc gur uvyy,
- Gb srgpu n cnvl bs jngre,
- Wnpx sryy qbja naq oebxr uvf pebja,
- Naq Wvyy pnzr ghzoyvat nsgre.

Code	A	B	C	D	E	F	G	H	I	J	K	L	M
Letter	N						T			W			
Code	N	O	P	Q	R	S	T	U	V	W	X	Y	Z
Letter				D					I		K	L	M

Solution:

> Jack and Jill went up the hill,
> To fetch a pail of water,
> Jack fell down and broke his crown,
> And Jill came tumbling after

Code	A	B	C	D	E	F	G	H	I	J	K	L	M
Letter	N	O	P	Q	R	S	T	U	V	W	X	Y	Z
Code	N	O	P	Q	R	S	T	U	V	W	X	Y	Z
Letter	A	B	C	D	E	F	G	H	I	J	K	L	M

Double or quit

- Give students a number as a starting point.
- Then get them to double that number and keep doubling the answer.
- See how far they can get by doubling the number.

First to seven

- Prepare a deck of cards that contains seven sets of seven cards.
- The seven cards in each set will relate to a specific topic and will have different words to do with that specific topic on each card. There will be seven different topics making a total of 49 cards.
- Add in three jokers to make a total of 52 cards.
- For example, a geography deck of cards could have seven cards to do with volcanoes (magma, lava, cone, crater, caldera, pyroclast and flow), seven to do with earthquakes (richter, epicentre, aftershock, plates, shockwaves, secondary damage, fault zones), seven to do with rivers (stream, confluence, tributary, source, meander, delta, waterfall), seven to do with glaciation (arête, moraine, tarn, cirque, crevasse, hanging valley, peak), seven to do with deserts (wadis, onion weathering, seif dunes, mesa,

butte, barchan dunes, cactus), seven to do with caves (stalagmite, stalactite, cavern, pillar, bedding planes, limestone, joints), and seven to do with rocks (igneous, sedimentary, metamorphic, granite, limestone, slate, impermeable) plus three jokers.

- Students form into groups of four to play the game.
- The 52 cards are shuffled and seven cards are dealt to each student.
- The rest of the cards are left in the centre face down – with one card turned up.
- Player 1 picks up either the upturned card or a card from the top of the face-down pack.
- They then place one card on the upturned pile.
- Each player does the same in turn until one player gets a complete set – seven cards with sets of words that all relate to the same topic.
- When they get a complete set they shout 'First to seven'. The game continues until the other three players complete their sets.
- If a joker is picked up this is a wild card that can be used as part of any set.
- The same could be done in English using seven plays or books and listing seven characters from each play/book or using seven poems and cutting them into seven strips which are then placed on playing cards.

Initial confusions

- Write up the initials and numbers in the left-hand column below and get the students to replace the letters with words.
- Do the first one as an example.
- Students should form groups of two, three or four to identify all the phrases that can be made from the initials and numbers.

12 S of the Z	(12 Signs of the Zodiac)
366 D in a LY	(366 Days in a Leap Year)
26 L in the A	(26 Letters in the Alphabet)
7 C of the R	(7 Colours of the Rainbow)
LO in 2012	(London Olympics in 2012)
52 W in a Y	(52 Weeks in a Year)
1440 M in a D	(1440 Minutes in a Day)
SR of 81 is 9	(Square Root of 81 is 9)
39 S by JB	(39 Steps by John Buchan)
HP and the G of F by JKR	(Harry Potter and the Goblet of Fire by JK Rowling)
6 W of H the 8	(6 Wives of Henry V111)
12 M in a Y	(12 Months in a Year)
1000 M in a KM	(1000 Metres in a Kilometre)
3 BM	(3 Blind Mice)
5 V in the A	(5 Vowels in the Alphabet)
100 P in a P	(100 Pennies in a Pound)
1 2 3 4 5 O I C A F A	(1 2 3 4 5 Once I Caught A Fish Alive)
24 H in a D	(24 Hours in a Day)
3 F in a Y	(3 Feet in a Yard)
G and the 3 B	(Goldilocks and the 3 Bears)

Magic numbers

- Ask the students to write down a number between one and 20.
- Then ask them to double it and add 14.
- Then they must divide their answer by two.
- Then take away their original number.
- No matter what number they chose in the first place they should be left with seven.

Solution:

To prove that the answer will always be seven no matter which number between one and 20 you choose, use the algebraic solution below:

- Let your number be N.
- Double it and add 14: $2N + 14$
- Divide your answer by two: $(2N + 14) / 2 = N + 7$
- Take away your original number: $N + 7 - N = 7$
- Your answer will always be seven no matter what number you choose.

Think of a number

- Ask the students to think of a number from one to ten.
- Then they must multiply that number by nine.
- If their number is a two-digit number they must add the digits together.
- Then subtract five.
- Ask them to determine which letter in the alphabet corresponds to their last number (for example 1 = A, 2 = B, etc.).
- Then they should think of a country that starts with that letter.
- They should then think of an animal beginning with the last letter of that country.
- Then think of a fruit that starts with the last letter of their animal.
- Ask them if they were thinking of a kangaroo in Denmark eating an orange.
- The majority of students will have chosen the above.

Solution:

- No matter which number is chosen the number left will always be four. Most people will then choose Denmark as their country, koala or kangaroo as their animal and orange or apple as their fruit.

Magic squares

- By using every number from two to ten complete the magic square below so that every horizontal, vertical and diagonal line adds up to 18.

		7
	6	
	4	

Solution:

3	8	7
10	6	2
5	4	9

- This time use every number from one to 16 to complete the magic square so that every horizontal, vertical and diagonal line adds up to 34.

		4	
2	12		
	3	14	
16			

Solution:

7	13	4	10
2	12	5	15
9	3	14	8
16	6	11	1

Mobile proverbs

- A proverb is a short and simple saying which is based on a common fact or observation. For example 'Better late than never'.
- There are four proverbs below, hidden in a code using numbers from a mobile phone pad.
- If the number in the code is a two then the letter could be a, b or c
- If the number is a six then the letter could be m, n or o.
- Try to identify the proverbs using the mobile handset below.

	2 abc	3 def
4 ghi	5 jkl	6 mno
7 pqrs	8 tuv	9 wxyz

Proverbs:

- 77433 26637 233673 2 3255
- 36789 8377357 6253 843 6678 66473
- 2 6477 47 27 4663 27 2 6453
- 866 6269 26657 77645 843 27684

Solutions:

- Pride comes before a fall
- Empty vessels make the most noise
- A miss is as good as a mile
- Too many cooks spoil the broth

Months of the year

- Get students to recite the months of the year January to December.
- Then get them to recite the months in reverse order December to January.
- Then in alphabetical order (April, August, December, February, January, July, June, March, May, November, October, September).

Muddled letters

- Can you unscramble the letters to make the names of towns and cities in England and Wales?
  - Rid caff
  - Ham grim bin
  - Old non
  - Tense charm
  - Tee rex
  - Dig near
  - Lop a block
  - Kyro
  - Edsel
  - Vored

Solutions:

- Cardiff
- Birmingham
- London
- Manchester
- Exeter
- Reading
- Blackpool

- York
- Leeds
- Dover
- You could also jumble up a list of key words to do with your subject.
- Maths: Love mu (Volume), Hag or pasty (Pythagoras), Quiet as no (Equations).
- Science: Salty cat (Catalyst), Meet len (Element), Knit ice (Kinetic).
- History: Open loan (Napoleon), No lens (Nelson), Gawky fuse – two words (Guy Fawkes).
- English authors: Seek a phrase (Shakespeare), Sick end (Dickens), Wroth sword (Wordsworth).

Spotlight

- A student comes to the front of the class and stands in an imaginary spotlight.
- All other students turn to the back of their books or use a scrap of paper and list the numbers one to ten.
- The teacher asks ten questions to the spotlight student. They answer each one out loud.
- After each answer the rest of the students individually decide if it was right (a tick), wrong (a cross) or weren't sure (?).
- The teacher in conclusion goes through the answers with the class and then checks to see who predicted the most correct responses to the spotlight student's answers.

Bridge activities

- In groups of four, get the students to list key words from last lesson, write them down then pass them on to the next group who then add further words.
- Ask students to visually represent their last lesson.
- Ask students to write a one-minute essay on what they have learnt.
- What am I? Either student or teacher chooses to be one 'thing' from last lesson. The group tries to identify the 'thing' by asking questions.
- Conduct a review by having learners stand in a circle. One asks a question and throws a ball. Whoever catches it answers a question and asks the next one.

Tearing off a strip (bridge to last lesson)

- Make a list of 21 key words to do with a topic.
- Give students a narrow strip of paper and get them to fold it into eight boxes.
- Then get students to select and write one word in each box.
- You then call out words from the list randomly and students tear off the word if it is at the top or bottom of their list.
- The first student to have torn off each word is the winner.
- Then get students in pairs and get them to stand back-to-back.
- In turn they should write the word using fingertip only on their partner's back.
- As soon as their partner identifies the word they then swap roles.
- This goes on until all 16 words (eight each) have been identified.
- The first group to finish wins.

For example:

RIA	SPIT	CONFLUENCE
ESTUARY	TOMBOLA	LBP
CLIFF	BAY	LONGSHIRE DRIFT
BEACH	HEADLAND	CUSP
RAISED BEACH	CAVE	NOTCH
GROYNE	WAVE	BAR
CURRENT	PEBBLES	TIDE

Brain breaks

When we first meet a group of students it is essential to establish rules and routines, to agree protocols for different types of work, how to manage transition and agree group structures for various activities. Setting the big picture at the beginning and chunking down the session into smaller components can help the disaffected and disengaged in particular. Brain breaks are very useful intermission moments to place in a session when energy levels are dipping and concentration is waning/lapsing. The more we can get learners active with their learning the more they are likely to engage. Brain breaks involve movements which link the left and right side of the brain and develop improved electrical firings across the corpus callosum, a connecting cord between those two sides. Our brain appears to be a better problem solver when we use both sides so we need to keep them active. Just by standing for an activity, 15 per cent more oxygen is fed to the brain. Physical movement actively increases the oxygen in the blood stream.

Dryden and Vos (2005) in quoting research, support this notion. They stated that working with dyslexic students over an eight-week period and using brain breaks for one afternoon per week over that period, 73 per cent of students showed significant improvement in three out of six learning abilities tested.

In Chapter 4 we outlined further benefits of brain breaks to open up neural pathways in the brains of students with under-developed spindle cells. Scientists have challenged elements of the stated benefits of brain breaks stating that in education neuromyths and pseudoscientific explanations abound. They challenge much of the brain theory and suggest that some of the theories are contradicted by scientific knowledge. Despite these challenges, brain breaks do have numerous benefits, which were stated earlier in the chapter. A whole range of brain breaks and starter activities can be found at www.brainbreaks.co.uk and a number have been taken from Vizard (2009), *Brain Breaks, Starter Activities and Fillers*.

Some examples of brain breaks are given below.

Sitting aerobics

- Sitting and running on the spot – while seated, students move their legs as though running on the spot.
- Swimming – while sitting, get the students to do four different swimming strokes and movements with each arm and leg – right-hand breaststroke motion, left-hand backstroke and then add one foot doing a different swimming kick and the other doing a different kick movement.

Finger aerobics

Get students to:

- Sit face-to-face with their partner at a desk.
- Get them to place their hands palm down on the desk.
- Take it in turns to lift different fingers off the desk.
- Build up a sequence of five lifts (ten between both students) and repeat the same sequence five times.
- Change routine by adding in taps, bends and big stretches of the finger.
- One person can then become an aerobics instructor and the other person has to do as they demonstrate.

Double doodles/palm-to-palm

Get students to:

- Doodle a shape in the air with one hand.
- Doodle in the air the same shape with both hands.
- Write a word in the air using one and then both hands.
- Join hands with a partner, palm-to-palm.
  - One student then writes their first name in the air using their right hand which results in their partner following those movements with their left hand. Partners then swap roles.
  - Both students should then write their names simultaneously in the air palm-to-palm.

New vocabulary

- Practise new vocabulary and lesson terms by asking students to write them in the air with their elbow and head. Then with their legs and hips whilst standing.

Figure it out

Ask students to follow these instructions:

- Sitting, rotate your right foot in a clockwise direction.
- After ten seconds keep your foot moving and simultaneously get your right hand to draw a figure of 6 in the air from the top down.
- As you move your hand you will notice that your foot reverses its direction and moves anti-clockwise.
- This is because the control centre for the right hand and foot are located close together on the left side of the brain.
- When the hand moves in the opposite direction to the foot then a short circuit or override function operates and the foot changes direction.
- The hand rules for survival.

Cross crawling/crossover dancing

- Get students to march slowly on the spot, bringing their left knee up to meet their right wrist (and vice versa).
- Motor movements that involve both sides of the body in this way simultaneously engage both hemispheres of the neo-cortex and stimulate communication between the left and right sides of the brain via the corpus callosum.

Body-part counting

- Allocate numbers one to nine to different body parts.
- For example, number one = nose, two = right ankle, three = left elbow, four = right knee, five = left ear, six = right elbow, seven = left knee, eight = left ankle, and nine = right ear.
- Give the group counting exercises one to nine and nine to one by going to the appropriate body part. Then do some simple addition: 1 + 3 + 5 = 9

Figures of 8

Encourage students to:

- Draw a figure of 8 lying on its side in the air with their writing hand – repeat this five times.
- Do the same with their non-writing hand.
- Now attempt this activity using both hands simultaneously.

Some other variations of this activity could include:

- **Elbow 8s**:
  - Draw figures of 8 with each elbow in turn.
  - Focus their gaze on their elbow as they turn their upper body to the rear, finally centring the 8 over the middle of their tailbone.
- **Shoulder 8s**:
  - Rotate both shoulders simultaneously in a figure of 8.

- **Whole-body 8s:**
  - ○ Both elbows doing 8s simultaneously while the top half of their body rotates 90 degrees to the left and then to the right.
- **Fingertips 8s:**
  - ○ Use both of their fingertips to trace figures of 8 in the air at the same time.
- **Clicking fingers 8s:**
  - ○ Click their fingers on both hands whilst making a figure 8 shape.

Air graphs

- Give students equations of line graphs on PowerPoint and get the whole group to stand and show the direction of the graph line using right and left hands. For example the graph $y = x$ will be a straight line running from bottom left to top right and the graph $y = 3 - x$ will be a straight line running from top left to bottom right.

Case Study

In one north-east England college of FE learners of all ages engage in brain breaks at the beginning and during sessions. It is a clear part of every member of staff's lesson planning. Each subject division produce their own 'brain warm-up booklet' which contain numerous brain warm-ups. Many are used at the start of the lesson to get learners into the frame of mind to learn which leads to more effective learning. Students of all ages engage with these activities and look forward to them at the beginning of the session or during the session.

Cooperative learning

Cooperative learning is an approach that gets students to work together in specific groups and variable groups that gives them a responsibility for their learning and involves an element of peer teaching.

Restructuring the way work is presented to learners can help. By using cooperative learning techniques we can better engage all students and certainly those who are disengaged or disaffected. Cooperative learning is highly effective academically and socially. The lesson is structured so that each student has a vested interest in each other's learning as well as their own. When regularly used, this approach can improve students' achievement by at least one grade.

Why does cooperative learning work?

It develops students academically and socially and allows students to learn by doing, is task-based and fun. Self-esteem of disaffected students is raised and they feel empowered. Some of its features and effects include:

- learning by doing/explaining (active learning)
- developing role/responsibility
- task-based – clear
- fun
- use of peer teaching
- use of group clarification – feedback; clearing up misconceptions/misunderstandings
- empowering
- improves self-esteem.

Strengths of cooperative learning

- increased learning takes place because learners take responsibility for their learning
- level of challenge is increased
- social skills are developed
- relationship with teacher is improved
- students are fully involved
- they have ownership of their learning
- high levels of reasoning are used
- generation of new ideas/creativity
- curiosity/motivation improved.

Weaknesses of cooperative learning

- risky – as it can possibly generate a lot of noise and there is the potential for students with behaviour problems to disengage
- does it work with all disaffected students?
- takes a lot of preparation time
- there is an assumption that students have the necessary skill level to work independently
- this approach may be strange to them.

Cooperative learning must be structured so that:

- groups sink or swim together
- students have a goal to learn and a goal to help others in the group to learn.

Cooperative learning groups

There are a number of ways to group learners for cooperative learning activities. These are:

Jigsaw groupings

Below are four ways that students could be grouped to develop cooperative learning.

1. Peer teaching

- Split the class into groups of five; each member of the group is given the number one, two, three, four or five.
- Each group studies a different area of a topic that has been studied in the classroom.
- Then the groups are regrouped by putting all the ones together, all the twos together and so on.
- Each person in the group teaches the rest of the group their topic.

2. Specialists

- Split the class into groups of five.
- Each group studies five different areas or answers five questions.
- Each group is given five different coloured pieces of paper – red, blue, green, yellow and orange.
- Each area studied has a colour attached to it and each member of the group is given an area and its associated colour.
- After 15 minutes students regroup with all the reds sitting together, etc.
- They then come up with the best answer from the information provided by the five groups.

3. In the zone

- Divide the room into five information points on a topic. For example – book area, computers, role-play area, teacher in role-play area for question and answer, leaflets and posters.
- Divide the students into groups of five.
- Each group sends a student to the different areas to gain information required by the task.
- Each group is given a must/should/could do list.
- Each group produces a report or gives a short presentation at the end.

4. Team event

- The class is divided up into teams.
- The teams have to come up with results.
- Different documents are given to different team members.
- Each team should have:
  - a project manager
  - a learning checker – ensure all group able to explain the work, must score seven out of ten as a group
  - a vocabulary chief – vocabulary sheet containing key words and meanings
  - a scribe
  - worker ants.
- At the end of the task the group conducts an evaluation.

Practical examples of cooperative learning in action

Specific examples of cooperative learning activities are given below.

Jigsaw pieces

- Cut up six different postcard scenes or pictures.
- Cut each card into at least ten pieces.
- Put four pieces of each image into an envelope with a photocopy of the picture to which these pieces belong.
- Jumble up the remaining pieces and put them into each envelope so that there are no more than ten pieces in each envelope.
- Divide the class into groups of four.
- Each group has to complete a postcard by swapping jigsaw pieces with other groups.
- The first group to complete their picture is the winner.
- This develops a cooperative learning approach and ensures students negotiate with each other. It also helps to develop mathematical and spatial intelligence.

Timeline

- Give students cards with dates written on them.
- Separately, give them cards with historical events that occurred on those dates.
- Ask them to match up the cards.

Events/dates could include:

- Henry VIII came to the throne in 1509
- Battle of Hastings 1066
- Alfred the Great came to the throne in 871
- The Great War (First World War) 1914–18
- English Civil War 1642–49
- Viking Invasions of Britain 899–1016
- Gunpowder Plot 1605
- Spanish Armada 1588
- 100 Years War 1337–1453
- Magna Carta 1215.

Hotseat activity

- Get students to research a topic e.g. Henry VIII, Brunel, Great Fire of London.
- They then have to talk for one minute without repetition, hesitation or deviation.
- The class listens for infringements of these rules and will challenge them.
- One point is given to the student challenging and one point is given to the student completing the minute.

Watch the Birdie – What a Picture!

- Get students into groups of five.
- One student from each group comes up to the front of the class and studies a picture for 30 seconds and then goes back and draws what they remember or tells group members the detail.
- Each group member goes up to look at the picture and add to the detail.
- Each group member then displays their picture as you would in an art gallery and you can discuss with the group what has been missed.

Dice throw

- Get students into groups of six.
- Each group has a dice.
- Prepare cards numbered one to six.
- Each group member is issued with one of these cards.
- Prepare cards A, B, C, D, E and F with six cards in each set.
- Put the letter on top of each card and on the face-down side write a question to do with a topic you have been studying.
- All six cards for each set must have questions to do with the same topic.
- Each set of six is a different topic.
- Player 1 shakes a dice – the number that is indicated on the dice relates to the person who is to answer the question.
- For example, if six is thrown, the player with the number six card takes the top card from the centre and answers the question.
- They then throw the dice and the number shown indicates the next player to play.
- For each correct answer one point is awarded to the player.
- At the end the group decides the connection between each set of cards.

English monarchs

- Write the name of one monarch on each card and get students to place these monarchs in the order they were on the throne:
  - William IV
  - Athelstan
  - Mary I
  - Anne
  - Canute The Dane
  - Ethelwulf
  - Harold I
  - John
  - Edward VII
  - Alfred The Great
  - Jane
  - William I
  - Victoria

- William III and Mary II
- James I [VI of Scotland].

Answers:

- Ethelwulf (839–58)
- Alfred The Great (871–99)
- Athelstan (924–39)
- Canute The Dane (1017–35)
- Harold I (1035–40)
- William I (1066–87)
- John (1199–1216)
- Jane (1553–54)
- Mary I (1553–58)
- James I [VI of Scotland] (1603–25)
- Oliver Cromwell (1653–58)
- William III and Mary II (1689–1702)
- Anne (1702–14)
- William IV (1830–37)
- Victoria (1837–1901)
- Edward VII (1901–10).

Backed up

- Students sit on chairs back-to-back.
- Student A selects an illustration from a geography textbook and describes it to Student B who draws it from their description.
- Student B can ask questions to help them.
- Student A is expected to be cooperative and helpful.
- Pictures could show maps, cross-sections, volcanic-cone diagrams or physical and cityscape features.

People maps

- Write place names/features onto separate pieces of card.
- Then get groups of students to construct a people map by standing group members in correct positions relative to one another.

Set 1 – United Kingdom

Llandudno	Newcastle	M5 Motorway
Mount Snowdon	Edinburgh	Bristol
Cardiff	Glasgow	River Severn
Manchester	Penzance	River Thames
Pennines	Plymouth	London
Leeds	Dartmoor	Firth of the Forth
Durham	Cairngorms	Ben Nevis

Set 2 – Japan

Hokkaido	Honshu	Shikoku
Kyushu	Kobe	Tokyo
Sapporo	Nagasaki	Mount Fuji
Sea of Japan	Pacific Ocean	

Mountains

- Get the students to place the following mountains in height order, from smallest to highest.
- Students could stick cards on the wall in height order or get themselves to represent each mountain with the highest mountain standing and the lowest person lying on the floor.
  - Kilimanjaro
  - Vinson Massif (Antarctica)
  - Scafell Pike
  - Everest
  - Mc Kinley (Alaska)
  - Ben Nevis
  - Snowdon
  - Mont Blanc
  - Aconcagua (Andes)

Answers:

- Everest   (1 – 8,848m)
- Aconcagua (Andes)   (2 – 6,960m)
- Mc Kinley (Alaska)   (3 – 6,194m)
- Kilimanjaro   (4 – 5,888m)
- Vinson Massif (Antarctica)   (5 – 5,139m)
- Mont Blanc   (6 – 4,810m)
- Ben Nevis   (7 – 1,347m)
- Snowdon   (8 – 1,085m)
- Scafell Pike   (9 – 978m)

Water cycle

- Place each numbered statement onto separate pieces of card.
- Then get students to rearrange these sentences, which describe the water cycle, into their correct order:

  [a] Condensation is when invisible water vapour turns into water droplets.

  [b] The sun heats up the earth.

  [c] The sun is virtually overhead at the equator all the year round.

  [d] As the droplets touch each other they join together and get heavier.

  [e] This is known as convectional rain.

  [f] As the air rises it cools.

  [g] The water turns into invisible water vapour.

  [h] Eventually they get too heavy and fall to the ground as heavy rain.

  [i] The droplets are light enough to float in the sky as clouds.

  [j] Hot air currents are known as convection currents.

  [k] The water vapour rises on hot air currents.

  [l] Any moisture on the earth's surface is evaporated.

  [m] Eventually it cools so much that condensation takes place.

Answers:

1. [c] The sun is virtually overhead at the equator all the year round.
2. [b] The sun heats up the earth.
3. [l] Any moisture on the earth's surface is evaporated.
4. [g] The water turns into invisible water vapour.
5. [k] The water vapour rises on hot air currents.
6. [j] Hot air currents are known as convection currents.
7. [f] As the air rises it cools.
8. [m] Eventually it cools so much that condensation takes place.
9. [a] Condensation is when invisible water vapour turns into water droplets.
10. [i] The droplets are light enough to float in the sky as clouds.
11. [d] As the droplets touch each other they join together and get heavier.
12. [h] Eventually they get too heavy and fall to the ground as heavy rain.
13. [e] This is known as convectional rain.

The elevens game

- The object of this game is not to say a number that is a multiple of 11.
- Ask all the students to stand up.
- Each student is allowed to say one, two or three consecutive numbers.
- The students take it in turns to say their numbers starting with the number one.
- Each student who says the number 11 or a multiple of the number 11 sits down.
- The game continues until the last person is left standing.
- An example of this could be:

1st person	'1, 2, 3'
2nd person	'4'
3rd person	'5, 6'
4th person	'7, 8, 9'
5th person	'10'
6th person	'11' (this person is now eliminated)
7th person	'12, 13'
8th person	'14, 15, 16'
9th person	'17, 18, 19'
10th person	'20, 21'
11th person	'22' (this person is eliminated)
12th person	'23' . . .

and so on.

- It is a game of strategy and the students will eventually work out how many numbers to say to avoid being eliminated.

Key points

Key points to think about from this chapter are:

- starter activities can be used to help focus disengaged and disaffected students at the beginning of the lesson
- brain breaks – intermissions in sessions to increase oxygen to the brain and electrical firings across left- and right-side of the brain; also act as an outlet for disaffected students who are kinaesthetic
- cooperative learning strategies to engage students and ensure they have a vested interest in their own and other students' learning.

Helping students to self-manage their behaviour

9

Many students bring a lot of emotional baggage with them to school. Because of the difficulties they face at home, or in the community with the challenge of gangs, or the difficulties they face with their learning, and the mixed messages they receive from the media, they arrive severely disrupted. There has often been an absence of a primary caretaker in those important early years and an absence of a supportive extended family. It is important to help these students by raising their self-esteem, resilience and ability to cope.

Many students who are disengaged and disaffected need help and support to manage their behaviour. They are prone to act out their anger and are likely to have angry outbursts. In this chapter I want to look at ways we can get students to identify the triggers that make them angry and spot the signs in themselves that they are about to become angry. Then I would like to outline approaches that learners can use to manage their own behaviour.

Triggers that are likely to make students angry

Below are some of the key triggers to anger:

- differences of opinion
- lack of tolerance of diversity
- the need to be right
- various types of rage – queue rage, road rage
- territorial issues – another student getting too close and invading the 50cm personal space bubble we all have; territory in class; turf wars between gangs
- people not listening to you – using communication blockers
- self-defence – defending close friends and family
- shadow – seeing something in another person that you don't like in yourself, therefore you attack it

- displacement – directing anger towards someone else, either because of the need to act out, or because they have a trait, physical appearance or vocal tone that the student does not like.

Signs students show when they are about to become angry

- they appear agitated
- they appear fidgety
- their face colour deepens and then goes pale as blood drains from their head and goes to their arms and legs for the fight or flight response
- their breathing quickens
- their pupils dilate
- they may speak faster and louder
- they move more quickly and have rapid movements
- their muscles tense
- their face may contort
- they may have hunched shoulders
- they are more easily distractible and lack focus.

Approaches to help students manage their behaviour

Having helped students to identify the triggers that cause them to become angry and display inappropriate behaviour and the physical signs that they are about to become angry, it is important to develop skills and strategies to help them. Students with low self-esteem can become very defensive so developing a form of impulse control is key – thinking about the possible consequences of their action. We need to get them to apply their brain brake – introduce a time delay between feeling and action – thus allowing a period of time for reflection.

Students who are disengaged are often rigid in their thinking and display a lack of empathy. They have low self-esteem and fragile egos. We need to work to reframe their negative feelings. We also need to develop problem-solving strategies.

The following are strategies that I would use with students who have behaviour and anger management issues:

- Get them to reflect on what anger is.
- Get them to identify sources of conflict and anger in their lives.
- Help them to develop impulse controls – get them to stop and think about reactions to situations. Use an imaginary DVD player pause button – go into freeze-frame mode. Get them to reflect on the situation, what their reaction is likely to be and the consequences of that action. What can you and others gain and lose from this action?
- To protect against hurtful comments get them to use an imaginary shield to deflect the comments and protect themselves. Encourage students to build an imaginary glass wall between themselves and the

person making the negative comments. Ask the students to visualize an imaginary tortoise shell into which they can go to shield and protect themselves.

- Ask students to break down situations that might trigger an angry response into a number of segments:
  - students should be encouraged to attempt to define the problem
  - think about alternative solutions to the situation
  - evaluate the alternatives and find the best one to use
  - they should avoid blaming the other person
  - aim for a win-win situation, not a win-lose situation.
- Consider the importance of body language and vocal tone and command in interactions. These are some points to reflect upon with students:
  - Open body language needed.
  - Positioning – standing at right angles to the person to avoid too much eye contact.
  - Remember we all have a 50cm personal space bubble around us, which we do not like people to move inside. When we are angry the space bubble is larger. Respect that and stand at an appropriate distance.
  - Posture is important – stand with an upright posture. Make firm gestures.
  - Ensure you are calm but firm in vocal delivery. Speak at the lower end of your vocal range to appear more confident and authoritative.
  - Speak slowly, use short scripts.
  - Manage gestures and body switches. Try to minimize movements as these can inflame.
- Students should, through role play, practise strategies to use in managing disagreements, arguments and conflicts successfully. Give them a range of scenarios to consider. Dramatherapy is also a useful approach to use; through music and drama we can help students to understand how to identify signs of anger and how to control their feelings. We can also give them an active vocabulary to use to negotiate in such situations.
- Get them to develop selective listening – it is possible to block out some of the negative statements made by the other person in a dispute.
- Develop assertiveness techniques with them. Assertiveness helps us to communicate clearly and with confidence. In helping disaffected students to engage we need to develop some of the following qualities of an assertive person. They:
  - can decide what they want and ask clearly for it
  - listen well
  - are aware of non-verbal communication
  - will give an outward appearance of being calm and relaxed
  - do not bottle up feelings
  - can express positive and negative thoughts
  - can take and give compliments and fair criticism
  - can cope with 'put-downs' and have developed the fogging technique to use in such circumstances.
- Give advice on responding to negative statements. Communicate that it is important not to be defensive, show upset or to argue back. If the statement is true, agree.
  'You noticed.'
  'I agree.'
  'That's right.'
  If it is not true you can say:

'That is your opinion.'

'You could be right.'

'It could be true.'

- Give students advice on how to deal with criticism – 'Agree with criticism and watch it go away'. Develop 'I' statements that explain in an assertive manner the effects of another person's behaviour. 'When you (behaviour), I feel upset (feeling) because I cannot work (effect). I would like you to (proposed solution).'

- Lessening/managing anger with these strategies:
  - ○ Visualization – Get students to imagine a special place, a quiet countryside area (river, woodland), holiday location when they felt good and had a very special feeling. Because they were in a nice location or on holiday they were probably happy and in a relaxed state. Get students to focus on the image and the feeling. Get them to use a large magnifying glass to enlarge the scene to make the colours bright and to intensify the feeling. This can have a calming influence. This is because it anchors you and your brain in a location where you felt good. Just visualizing the location makes you feel good. Often it is good to get students to touch their knee, wrist, elbow or press thumb and forefinger together when visualizing a scene and remembering the intense positive feeling and image. Later when they feel anger rising, it is often sufficient to touch their knee, wrist, elbow or press thumb and forefinger together for the positive scene to return and thereby create a more relaxed state. The mind associates the feeling with that particular gesture and movement.
  - ○ Learning to breathe for relaxation. You can encourage students to develop a deep-breathing cycle which will help them to relax. When breathing in, get students to expand their chest slowly and push out their stomach which creates more space for the lungs to expand. Then get the students to follow this sequence. Breathe in through the nose for four seconds, hold breath for three seconds and then exhale through the mouth and be aware of the feeling you get as your lungs empty. Do this up to ten and back to one. This will mean there will have been 20 cycles of breathing in and out. This controlled breathing is relaxing and will release happy hormones (endorphins).
  - ○ When faced with difficult and confrontational situations get students to count to ten before responding, relax muscles and repeat, under the breath, 'calm, calm, calm'.
  - ○ Progressive muscle relaxation. Tense muscles in toes and then relax, go to calf muscles, buttocks, stomach, chest, arms, shoulders and neck and do the same. This relaxes and changes the mental state.
  - ○ Make the following objects available for students to use – stress balls, bean bags and objects to squeeze to reduce stress.
  - ○ Get students to use internal distraction techniques – recite the alphabet from Z to A, name the days of the week in German, sing a song.
  - ○ Encourage students to talk to themselves – use positive self-talk. Get students to list four or five statements that they can think of when faced with another person's anger. This will help them to diffuse the chances of conflict.
    - – 'My voice will stay quiet and calm even if I am screaming inside.'
    - – 'Who makes me angry? I am the only person who can make me angry.'
    - – 'An angry person says things they don't mean.'
    - – 'Angry people exaggerate when they are angry.'
    - – 'This person is displacing their anger on me – when it should be going elsewhere.'
    - – 'Stay calm and respond in a controlled way when an angry person makes negative and critical statements.'
    - – 'The time to negotiate with an angry person is later – when their anger has subsided.'

Top Tip

The development of relaxation techniques in students is essential through:

- visualization
- using breathing techniques
- counting to ten
- progressive muscle relaxation
- using distraction techniques
- using positive self-talk.

- Get students to reframe – students who behave badly tend to have extremely low self-esteem and a very negative self-image; they think that 'everyone in the world has it in for me'. This self-downing has been described as 'psychological junk mail'. It affects students' ability to cope. There is a need to reframe the problem, looking at it realistically and to get students to reframe the negatives into positives – looking for the good in every situation.
- The slightest look or nudge can cause extreme and angry reactions in many students. Because of low self-esteem they have very short fuses and can become very angry and confrontational with the slightest provocation. Working with learners we need to develop an alternative reaction when things occur. So if someone bumps into them for example you could explain that it may not be to pick a fight, but it could be because they stumbled or someone else pushed them.
- Developing active listening techniques in students so that they can communicate effectively is important. Many students are good at blocking communication by:
  - challenging
  - interrupting
  - dominating
  - accusing
  - criticizing
  - name-calling
  - contradicting
  - putting down.

  We need to develop the following active listening skills:
  - face the speaker
  - look the speaker in the eye
  - be attentive
  - nod and make sounds to show you are listening
  - do not fidget or interrupt
  - if you do not understand something wait until the speaker has finished explaining and then ask for clarification
  - try to feel what the speaker is feeling – develop empathy
  - at the end summarize what the speaker has said.

  In Chapter 3 we spoke about the importance of active listening. For example when meeting a person, listening to what they have to say and not flooding them with 'me, me, me' statements. Active listening is a key part to positive communication.
- Use time-out cards. When students are finding it difficult to cope in sessions they can be issued with a

time-out card for a limited period. The aim of the card is to enable them to leave a lesson when conditions are such that they may do something they will regret. For example – another student is winding them up so much that they may retaliate or the teacher may say something which may cause the student to become angry. When a student feels that they may have to leave a lesson, because they may explode, then they show the card to their teacher who lets them leave the room to cool off. The student is then expected to find a nominated member of staff who will spend time with the student discussing the causes of their problem at that time and will give them strategies to cope. The card is signed by the member of staff to show arrival and departure time.

- Circle time – When students experience problems in relationships with other students or staff, it can lead to conflict. It is a group discussion where feelings, hopes and experiences are discussed. Over a period of time resentment and anger may build which, if not dealt with, can lead to serious repercussions for the student and others with whom they may come into contact. Circle time can be a useful strategy. Students sit in a circle and discuss their problems and successes. Clear protocols/rules are established for the group. For example:
  - leave your baggage anger outside
  - everyone has the right to express their feelings without being put down
  - listen to the other person sharing
  - only one person to speak at any one time
  - sharing experiences and feelings openly is accepted by all group members
  - share time amongst the group equally
  - do not interrupt
  - you do not have to say anything
  - a positive atmosphere has to be maintained
  - group leader to thank everyone for their contribution.

  When managing circle time you need to describe what will happen. Remind students of the rules and then allow time for the circle to discuss issues. Sometimes you can form an outer circle who observe the inner circle when they are involved in the circle time discussions. After 15 minutes the inner circle moves to the outer circle to observe the next discussion (and the outer circle move to the inner circle and begin their discussions). At the end of each session it is important to summarize the discussion. At the end thank everyone for participating and keeping to the rules. Relax the group, be positive and make sure everyone is in the correct state physically and mentally to go to the next lesson.

- Goal setting and practise of skills. Working one-to-one with a student can help the student to manage and modify their behaviour by setting goals or targets. 'One small step' and 'a day at a time' would be key phrases to use. Setting easy to achieve targets and allowing opportunities to practise new patterns of behaviour in small steps would be good as this ensures success. Front-loaded reward systems are also important so that students are initially rewarded frequently for modification of their behaviour.

- Peer mediation – Getting a neutral third party to mediate and help settle conflict and disputes between students has been very successful in a number of institutions. This is a voluntary role and is not about making judgements as to who is right or wrong. The aim of the mediator is to help disputants resolve their conflict. Skills needed by the mediators are:
  - good listening and speaking skills
  - the ability to heed the views, needs and feelings of the disputants
  - the ability to find solutions – resolution skills.

  Peer mediation develops students' problem-solving ability and works because it empowers students to attempt to resolve conflict. It helps to develop a positive ethos where there is trust and open communication. There are also positive relationships. Former troublesome students have been found to be very effective mediators: 'poacher turned gamekeeper'. They have first-hand experience of disputes and enjoy taking on the responsibility of settling disputes through negotiation.

Case Study

> In one school in south-west England they have a Calm after the Storm centre (CATS centre) coordinated by the counsellor who works with a group of trained students, mentors and mediators. Students who are angry or are stressed and volatile, visit the centre at break times, and talk through key issues with the counsellor, mentor and mediators. The establishment of this centre has had a beneficial effect on disaffected students.

- When negative comments are being made a good way of getting students to feel better is getting them to imagine that they have blown a huge bubble into which they step. This energy bubble is strong, brightly coloured and acts as a force field. All the negative comments bounce off the bubble. It is a bit like the force shield on *Star Trek* surrounding the Starship Enterprise. They can't get to you. This engages the unconscious mind, which cannot determine what is reality and what is imaginary.

The range of strategies listed in this chapter will help to support disengaged students and help them to manage their behaviour more effectively.

Key points

> Key points to think about from this chapter are:
>
> - helping students to identify triggers to anger
> - ways to help students to identify the signs that they are becoming angry
> - approaches to help students to manage their own behaviour.

Managing disruptive, defiant and confrontational behaviour in individuals and groups

10

How often have we been working happily with a group of students when suddenly some extreme and challenging behaviour that has been triggered for no apparent reason is delivered by a particular student. Many learners who are disaffected and disengaged carry a lot of baggage, and extreme and challenging behaviour can be easily triggered in them. Their poor experiences in school can mean that they can feel extremely vulnerable.

In the first chapter I suggested a number of reasons that may be the cause of aggressive and confrontational behaviour. Students arrive disrupted by their confusing world. The lack of care, nurture and modelling of self-control in the home leads to aggression as a typical response. Behaviour can also be more confrontational because young people are turning to youth communities and gangs for support, role models and a sense of identity. Often violence and aggression are key elements of these groups.

The brain dimension relating to disruptive and confrontational behaviour

Vizard (2007a) suggests that the reptilian survival part of the brain located at the top of the spinal cord and at the base of the brain is the area that is triggered when there is a perception or threat of danger. When triggered it sends adrenalin and cortisol through our veins and gets us into a state of readiness – a code red state. It drains blood from the brain and this extra blood is sent to the muscles in the arms and legs ready for a fight or flight response which is key to our survival. Citing work by Fisher (2005), Vizard suggests that 'deep-seated unresolved traumatic events in our life' (Fisher 2005, p. 48) can remain stored in our brains, and act as triggers for over-reactions to situations at a later period of time. So learners who have had traumatic experiences when younger can have a number of memories carried at a subconscious level. Because of this they are vulnerable and are likely to display unpredictable outbursts of extreme behaviour. Many learners are scared by their extreme outbursts and in Chapter 9 we looked at strategies we can give these learners to help them manage their behaviour. With more extreme behaviours students would need interventions and support from specialist external agencies.

If young people experience high levels of stress in early years, the cortisol can have a toxic effect on the social brain (as mentioned in Chapter 1). Also neural pathways develop which link the reptilian brain directly with the impulsive areas of the brain such as the amygdala. When faced with a problem, messages are sent to the reptilian part of the brain rather than to the thinking area – the neo-cortex – and can lead to inappropriate responses and a lack of self-control.

Research Zone

Australian scientists at the University of Melbourne have conducted research on 150 boys and girls aged 11–14 and filmed their behaviour. Then they gave the youngsters MRI brain scans. They found that the shape of the brain had an impact on extreme behaviours. The amygdala was found to be bigger in those youngsters who were prone to prolonged and aggressive arguments. These differences, thought to be linked to a growth spurt of the brain during adolescence, would affect behaviour later in life.

Mistaken goals of behaviour

Dreikurs et al. (1998) suggest that a misbehaving student has lost their belief that they can find belonging and recognition and believes that they will find acceptance through provocative behaviour by pursuing the mistaken goals of behaviour. He stated that there were four mistaken goals:

- to gain undue attention
- to seek power
- to seek revenge or to get even
- to display inadequacy.

Many disaffected students pursue a number of these goals often without being aware that they are doing it. Alfred Adler, a medical psychologist from Austria, also believed that students create conflict in order to get attention even though this may cause further problems. He suggested that each of the above maladaptive goals of behaviour reflected a lack of emotional awareness.

Birkett (2005, p. 56), when accounting for challenging and confrontational behaviour, suggests we need to see through the hidden agenda of students.

> Often, fear of allowing people to get close to them will mean that pupils with challenging behaviour use hostility and anti-social behaviour to keep you – and other people – at a distance. They are looking for a place to dump their accumulated internal anger, often inappropriately. That place may be you. Don't take things personally.

Students who display confrontational behaviour enjoy the oxygen of publicity that they get from performing in front of their peer group. It is also a way of emptying their stress buckets.

When managing disruptive, defiant and confrontational behaviour in individuals consider the following:

- Calm yourself before communicating with the person. Take a few deep breaths. You could use the breathing technique mentioned in Chapter 9.

> **Research Zone**
>
> Rogers (2000, p. 133) stated that Brad Bushman (Iowa State University) conducted a study of 600 people and 'he observed that those who had practised calmness before expressing their anger were less aggressive in their expression of anger'.

- Avoid having an emotional reaction to the confrontation. We need to keep our emotions in check throughout the interaction.
- Your initial response is key in a confrontational situation. Dix (2005, p. 52) states the importance of setting a rhythm by your initial response:

Your response to the first signs of a confrontation sets the rhythm of the rest of the discussion. Change your focus from being the speaker to the listener. While you are listening look at your own body language and soften it.

This relates back to some of the topics discussed in Chapter 3 (about Neuro-Linguistic Programming – and building rapport with students).

- It is important not to get hooked into a power struggle – remember who the adult is. It is your response that can lead to a de-escalation or an escalation of the confrontation.
- Try not to take it personally or become too defensive. Keep it in perspective.

 **Top Tip**

Your initial reaction can have a significant impact on the outcome. Practise listening, avoiding an emotional reaction and avoiding getting into a power struggle. And most importantly, don't take it personally.

- Listen to what the student is saying. Dix sums up the importance of active listening by saying 'you will find that the confrontation needs the fuel of an equally confrontational response to keep it escalating' (2005, p. 53). Through listening thoroughly you can be more effective at de-escalating situations.
- Respond to their feelings and not their actions. Try to be solution focused.
- When speaking to the students use a brief short script which addresses the issue. Make sure the message is clear. Prefacing with a positive statement. 'I liked your work last lesson. Today I want you to . . .'
- Positioning is key – standing at right angles to the student or alongside them may be less threatening. Remember that an angry student has a large personal space bubble around them. Normally the space bubble or zone of comfort is about 50cm around us. Standing inside that zone or too close with an angry student can exacerbate the situation. However, standing too far away might be seen as a sign of weakness. By standing in this position we are avoiding excessive eye contact as that is often threatening. Also remember that with some minority ethnic groups maintaining eye contact and staring are very disrespectful acts.
- Avoid too much movement as this can make the situation worse. Convey non-aggressive intentions with your body language.
- Show respect by reflecting on what they are saying and use pauses between responses.
- Vocal tone relating to your response is key. Try not to show nervousness. Raise your voice to get attention and then lower it into a firm, calm, measured tone. In relation to vocal tone it is important to avoid a domineering tone. This point is nicely reinforced by Michel de Montaigne, a famous writer and poet in the sixteenth century, who wrote 'he who establishes his argument by noise and command shows that his reason is weak'.
- Try to give out 'nuggets of praise' – catch 'em being good. Often we are just reactive and respond to their bad behaviour.
- Use certainty not severity when dealing with incidents. We often threaten sanctions but do not deliver – say what you mean, mean what you say.
- Do not try to resolve conflict when someone is still angry. Wait for a period of time, buy time out. Then discuss the matter later.

'Time cools, time clarifies, no mood can be maintained, quite unaltered through the course of hours' (Thomas Mann).

Case Study

In a Scottish school the additional needs department has set up a special nurture area. A behaviour support worker is available to support students who have become angry and confrontational in class. If students become aggressive they can take time out by showing a card to the teacher. They then go to the nurture room. In this room they have a calming environment:

- pastel shades used on walls
- softer lighting – lava lamp effect
- gentle music playing
- plants in the room which students look after
- goldfish in bowl which students look after
- a water feature with flowing water over a sphere
- soft chairs and lower tables
- outside there is a small garden planted by students growing bonsai plants.

Students come to this room and talk to the behaviour support worker who helps the student to calm down and to reflect on their behaviour before they negotiate the re-entry of the learner to the classroom.

- Sometimes we need to give a clear instruction and then move away from the student. If we remain with the student confrontation may continue and we move into a downward spiral. Make it obvious that you have a clear expectation that compliance will occur.
- Paradoxical instruction – Long (2007, p. 7) suggests that learners, when defiant and disruptive, often decide to walk away – a flight response. He recommends that we say to them 'That's OK. You go for a walk and we will talk about this later.' Through giving this instruction, Long suggests that 'the student is now not defying you but instead carrying out your instructions and not being defiant'.
- Dix (2005) says that students have a sophisticated defence armoury they use when confronted. Often they will use smirks or kick furniture across the room. He says: 'They are "chase me" behaviours designed to get an emotional response from the teacher. Don't ignore them but choose the right time to address them when the student has calmed down.' (2005, p. 54)
- We sometimes need to make a token concession – the 1 per cent technical error strategy. Acknowledge that we could be part of the problem.
    - 'It could have been dealt with better.'
    - 'I see it could be annoying to be told . . .'
- Sometimes when a student is angry they will say things they don't mean – they often displace their anger on you. Often it is best to let them have their say and to run out of steam before responding.

- Students sometimes need reassurance – use inclusive language: people get angry so it's OK to feel that way and we will certainly be able to find a solution.
- Avoid the 'oxygen of publicity' generated by public exchanges by perhaps moving closer to the student and using proximity and level – sitting next to the students and talking quietly about the issue or taking the discussion somewhere private (but not away from a third party, otherwise you may be vulnerable).
- Avoid an upward spiral of confrontational behaviour. Do not try to mirror their mood. For example if they shout avoid the temptation to shout louder. It is best to match the mood level while showing some heightened response.
- On some occasions, in contrast, it may be necessary to be assertive and use command statements if defiant or disruptive behaviour was being displayed in a workshop.
- Faupel et al. (1998) suggest we should encourage students and teacher to swap places – to 'step into my shoes or see it through my eyes'. This is where you have to explain the issue from the other person's viewpoint.
- Try to establish rapport with the student by matching and mirroring body language. With speech try to talk in similar sentence lengths, using the familiar phrases they use (within reason) and try to match their tone. Also match their sensory predicates mentioned in Top Tip in Chapter 1.
- Avoid power struggles with learners. Check your speech volume and ensure your body language is appropriate.
- We learnt in Chapter 7 about the importance of laughter and fun. Using humour in some situations can relieve tension.
- Distraction techniques can be used to break the cycle of confrontation. It is a way of getting their attention away from the conflict. For example 'Is that a flying saucer I have just seen flying across the sky?'
- Show that you are willing to accept a compromise, a solution that is acceptable to all and allows everyone to feel a winner. Making token concessions can be good, admit that they may have a point. Be generous next time if you win this time.
- Wrong-footing tactics are useful. Often learners behave in a particular way – they attempt to touch your hot button to get a response. Not behaving in the way they expect can wrong-foot them and knock them off balance.
- By thinking about typical types of disruptive, defiant and confrontational behaviour we can prepare short, scripted responses to these situations. Use body language and phrases you have rehearsed and successfully used previously.
- If a student says something inappropriate try to avoid reacting immediately. Use silence and take several deep breaths. This will give them an opportunity to change what they said.
- Always model the behaviour you expect to see. Avoid the 'bad day' syndrome where you display a confrontational style to students.
- If you find yourself being dominant, using threatening behaviour and making idle threats then you will have great difficulty in managing the situation. Use your brain brake impulse-control mechanism to avoid such behaviour in the future.
- If a student is intent on negative behaviour and is making negative comments thank them for their comments and tell them that you will discuss them at the end of the lesson! This will sow seeds of doubt and will keep them guessing as to what will happen. Their behaviour also did not get the expected response.

- If you are trying to talk to a student about an issue and they are blanking or ignoring you a useful script to use is: 'I needed to talk to you about . . . if you can't do so now I will need to see you later'. This implies that it will take place in their own time.
- Try to understand the triggers that cause some students to become confrontational.
- With students in confrontational situations we can use the pacing and leading techniques discussed in Chapter 3 – where we used the running alongside a train metaphor to describe pacing and leading.
- Asking students for their help is a good strategy to use when trying to diffuse conflict.
- When involved in managing conflict it is essential that we ensure that we repair and rebuild our relationship with them and we don't allow situations to fester.

Case Study

In one Pupil Referral Unit (PRU) in central England the headteacher ensures that there is a very clear structure and routine for all students. Each student is expected to follow the dress code and to wear the correct uniform.

In their classroom students are expected to be seated at separate tables. In order to minimize distractions the table is divided into two sections; one side of the table is an open space where they can complete their work whilst the other side contains two boxes, the first containing their exercise books and work and the other containing all the equipment they will need.

The headteacher has found that working initially on single tables with all the materials required has improved concentration and the work of the students. Many students previously wasted too much time by not having the necessary materials and work for the lesson and by wandering around and disturbing other students. There are occasions when different groupings of students are used for cooperative learning.

Disruptive, defiant and confrontational behaviour in groups

Many groups of students now offer high levels of challenge. Students who are disaffected and who have behavioural difficulties can work together to cause problems in the learning environment. It is a good way to avoid work and can gain them notoriety. This often fuels the behaviour. With challenging groups of students it is important to identify the roles played by group members. Each group member will have at least one key role to play in the group. In Chapter 3 I suggested, through group brain break activities, it is possible to identify the rapport leader – the person who is first to do the activity. Others watch and wait for their involvement before they engage. The rapport leader is likely to be an alpha male or alpha female in the group. Vizard (2007a, p. 87) in describing alpha males says:

they are likely to be physically bigger than their peers and will be of above-average intelligence . . . A parallel you may have seen in the animal kingdom would be the baboon that sits at the top of the baboon rock at the local zoo.

Alpha females show signs of being leaders from 6 to 7 years old. They use psychological strategies to dominate others. They do not use violence but a subtle form of undermining of confidence. Alpha females are very sarcastic and use stage whispers when discussing other students with their friends. They can be so sarcastic it has been suggested that metaphorically 'acid drips from their tongue as they speak'.

Moore (2006) stated that girls used rumour-mongering, social isolation and non-verbal communication as a powerful weapon to control others. The laddette culture has also developed the influence of the alpha female. It is important to identify these ring leaders and to get them onside by using rapport-building strategies identified in Chapter 3.

Identifying the roles played by group members is essential to help us manage those challenging behaviours. Often when groups come together there is quite a lot of challenging and confrontational behaviour as the group tries to develop its own hierarchy. Each student battles for supremacy to become the alpha male and alpha female. Tuckman (1965) suggested that there are four typical stages in group formation:

- forming – group not sure of structure
- storming – disagreements and conflicts between group members and subgroups that have formed
- norming – group is now quite cohesive and becomes more mature; rules are now established
- conforming – the group works well on problem-solving and conflicts are resolved.

It is important when managing groups initially that we understand that these are the phases that they will go through. We need to support these developments and offer team-building strategies to help with these developments.

Very young children are joining gangs. They often face pressure from their siblings and peers to join. A knowledge of gang culture is key to helping us manage the behaviour of groups. Some of the following things have been done by schools to help students at risk of gang membership:

- diversionary activities for gang members – late-night sporting activities
- students have been given the following skills:
  - clear communication in difficult situations
  - how to deal with bullying, identifying when adults need help, anger management and respect for others
  - role play
  - how to avoid drugs
  - how to set goals and behave responsibly

- o clear communication – verbal and non-verbal
- o how to resist peer pressure
- o recognizing anger in others and calming them
- o conflict resolution and consequences of fighting.

Schools that have been successful in managing the influence of gang culture have used LEAP (www.leaplinx.com), an organization that has been involved in schools, helping them to address youth conflict, helping students to handle conflicts and to deal with situations. Some strategies that we can use with disruptive, defiant and confrontational groups are as follows:

- Keep it in proportion – over-concern can impede creative thought.
- Try to identify the reasons for the behaviour:
  - o Why is it happening to me at this moment?
  - o What are the triggers?
  - o Use intelligence – roles played by group members.
- It is not personal – their behaviour is logical – it is the way for them to survive or manage life.
- Experiment – try small things to change the behaviour. Being too dramatic too soon could have a catastrophic effect.

Understanding the influence of gangs and the youth subculture on the behaviour of groups is essential. In Chapter 1 the influence of youth communities and gangs as alternative families was discussed. At about nine years of age students start to identify with particular groups as a result of friendships or because the group represents their interests. These subculture groups are less formal than many of the gangs that are common today. Some of the youth subculture groups are given below (names may vary from area to area):

- townie
- skater
- emo
- metal head
- nerd/geek
- goth
- glam
- outcase
- outcast.

Each of these groups has different dress codes, hairstyles, musical interests, hobbies and aspirations. An understanding of some of these are helpful when we are managing their behaviours. Gangs now impact upon the behaviour of groups in school. Often disaffected students are the most vulnerable and join gangs for the esteem it brings. The behaviour of many students is more challenging and defiant because of their gang membership. Turf warfare often based on cultural groups is breaking out in schools. Over 5 per cent of students are in or on the fringe of gang culture. This is a small number but their impact can be devastating and disproportionate. Some strategies we can use to try and reduce this percentage are:

- develop a positive group identity
- have mutually agreed rules
- chunk it down and signpost the session
- divide and rule – split troublesome groups and use these students as leaders
- use cooperative learning approaches and use jigsaw groupings so that they don't realize they have been split
- use drama, which engages students in discussing key issues and allows them a safe framework for experimenting with concepts and ideas
- give them lots of responsibilities, e.g. engage disaffected students in a student-run radio station.

Using the strategies outlined in this chapter you will be able to manage the disruptive, defiant and confrontational behaviour displayed by disaffected students more effectively.

Key points

> Key points to think about from this chapter are:
>
> - the brain dimension relating to disruptive and confrontational behaviour
> - mistaken goals of behaviour
> - key strategies to use when managing individual disruptive, defiant and confrontational behaviour
> - managing disruptive, defiant and confrontational behaviour in groups.

11 Developing a consistent approach to meet the needs of disaffected students

Students who are challenging and disaffected usually come from home environments where there is a lack of nurture, where firm boundaries do not exist. Their world is turbulent and disruptive. What these students need in school is an environment where there are firm boundaries, tough love and a consistent approach. Many Pupil Referral Units (PRUs) ensure that students work in an environment where there is a consistency of expectation, and clear, firm and predictable boundaries are in place.

If you track a student for a day in your own institution or talk to support staff (such as Teaching Assistants (TAs) and Learning Support Assistants (LSAs)) who work often with students or groups of students they may state there are inconsistencies in the way the same types of behaviour are managed from room to room. This can become very confusing for students, as they receive mixed messages from teacher to teacher.

Some schools which have higher levels of exclusion and have higher levels of disruptive behaviour can be negative learning environments where the interventions used are strongly sanction-led. The repertoire of behaviour management strategies used are often limited and there is a lot of premature upward referral by staff (students often pushed up the hierarchy of sanctions quickly with levels missed out completely). These regimes are reactive environments. As a result they are often negative environments in which to work with ever escalating levels of disruption.

Birkett (2005) states that to develop a positive model of behaviour management the institution needs to create a positive learning environment initially (refer to Chapter 5 in this book), which is likely to act as a preventative measure – where incidents of poor behaviour are less likely to occur. She then suggests there needs to be a management level where managing behaviour is delivered through classroom strategies, with the final level indicating how confrontational behaviour is managed. There are lower levels of confrontation and poor behaviour in institutions where a positive learning environment is developed from the outset. She emphasizes that in order for a school to be successful, it needs to be proactive and consistent in its approach to behaviour management.

There is a need for teams of staff working with students who are challenging and disaffected to develop a consistent approach to managing those groups.

Leaman (2005, p. 12) reinforces the importance of consistency and in particular how we need to deal consistently with incidents day-in day-out – we should not change our approach.

> Consistency is vital in developing trust and compliance. If your response to challenging behaviour is consistently calm, firm and thorough (i.e. you see things through), your students will recognize that you are able to remain in control of the classroom and that they will not 'get away with it'.

Through taking a consistent approach with disaffected students, it is possible to get them 'onside' and potentially limit the volatility of their negative behaviour.

It is important to have a clear idea of how to deal with the different types of challenging behaviour we meet. Students comment on how they view good staff as those who treat people equally.

I have worked over the years with a large number of schools throughout the UK on developing a consistent approach to managing behaviour within those institutions.

Case Study

Working with one group of lecturers in a FE college in sport and leisure we developed a consistency model for the subject team of staff to use with a particularly challenging group of students. This group of 16 year olds were causing all sorts of problems for staff by:

- arriving late
- not bringing the correct clothing and equipment
- not listening to instructions
- frequently challenging staff
- using bad language.

We worked together to identify the key behaviours and developed a consistency model using the approach below, which lists the five common behaviours and five behaviour management strategies for each. Once this had been produced the team of staff met and agreed how they would work with the students initially and which of the five areas of behaviour they would concentrate upon.

Over the four weeks the behaviour of group members improved dramatically – because all staff were managing those problem behaviours in a consistent manner.

The key challenging behaviours most frequently encountered by staff are low-order behaviours which occur day-in day-out and can be quite debilitating. One strategy that can be used to help deal with this is to arrange for staff to form into groups to discuss these behaviours and to develop strategies to use with each. Based on these strategies a consistency model for all staff to use could be developed. If all staff use these strategies then the behaviour is potentially better managed and students are more likely to conform. However, some situations do require flexibility.

Vizard (2007a) suggested that one approach to developing a consistency model is by using a 'jigsaw' technique. This technique involves all staff discussing the key challenging behaviours faced. The following steps can be taken in order to develop your own consistency model.

- Get all staff to discuss the key challenging behaviours they face and then agree a top five list of behaviours.
- Assign each behaviour a letter 'a–e'. For example behaviour 1 = 'a', behaviour 2 = 'b' and so on.
- Get staff to split into five groups of five. Within these groups assign a member of staff to each behaviour. (Teacher 1 in the group is given behaviour denoted by 'a', teacher 2 is given 'b' and so on.)
- Ask staff to discuss these behaviours in their groups and produce one strategy for each behaviour.
- Then change the groups around so that all staff assigned to the same behaviours sit together. (For example all people assigned behaviour 'a' sit together, all those assigned 'b' sit together and so on.)
- Then ask these new groups of five to decide upon three strategies for their designated behaviours from the list of five they have.
- Once decided, the strategies for each behaviour should be published as a consistency model. So there will be a sheet of A4 paper on which there are the five behaviours and three strategies for each.

Using this approach, behaviours can be modified, and disaffected learners who need consistency the most get it and can thrive in a structured, secure and certain environment.

Key points

> Key points to think about from this chapter are:
>
> - the importance of developing a consistent approach to managing the behaviour of disaffected students
> - an outline of how to develop a consistency model.

Appendix

Research zone

Office for National Statistics (ONS)/Department for Health (2008), 'Three Years On – A Survey of the Emotional Development and Well-being of Children and Young People' – Funded by the Department for Health and published by ONS.

This survey sampled children between 2004 and 2007 and reviewed factors likely to be associated with the onset or persistence of disorders and also considered factors which protected against the onset. The researchers initially surveyed 8,000 children aged 5–16 in 2004. They found that children suffer badly from divorce or parent break-up. A child whose parents split between 2004 and 2007 was four and a half times more likely to have developed an emotional disorder than one whose parents had stayed together. The full report is available at www.statistics.gov.uk.

The Prince's Trust (2008) – 'The Culture of Youth Communities' – a survey of 1,754 young people aged 14–25 years old found that young people were turning to groups and 'youth communities' for support rather than their parents as role models.

The Good Childhood Inquiry – Evidence Summary 5 on Health published by the Children's Society. This report is Part 5 of six thematic reports, which include Friends, Family, Learning, Lifestyle and Values. A wide range of individuals and organizations (academics, local authority, health professionals, teachers and students) have submitted evidence into the inquiry. It found that 300,000 children aged 11–15 have mental health problems. Over 1 million children aged 5–16 have a clinically recognizable mental disorder ranging from depression, anxiety and anorexia to violent delinquency.

The Tellus 3 Survey of children published by Ofsted (2008), the second national survey of children and young people aged 10–15 years of age, asked young people to report on how they feel in relation to the five areas of *Every Child Matters* (2003). It asked about how safe they feel, if they enjoy school, if they are happy and if the advice on sex and relationships is sufficient. The report highlighted that bullying was a significant problem and a large proportion of young people said their bodies/self-image was a source of worry. The Tellus 3 Survey (2008) is available from www.ofsted.gov.uk.

Useful websites

ADHD
www.addiss.co.uk – ADDISS – Attention Deficit Disorder Information and Support
www.add.org – Attention Deficit Disorder Association
www.cdc.gov/ncbddd/adhd – Information on ADHD from Department of Health and Human Services

Asperger Syndrome
www.aspergerinformation.org – website providing information for AS
www.aspergerssyndrome.org – Information about AS and autism

Dyslexia
www.bdadyslexia.org.uk – website providing information and advice on dyslexia
www.dyslexiaaction.org.uk – website for national charity Dyslexia Action
www.dyslexiatreatment.com – Dyslexia Treatment Centre

Dysgraphia
www.snapassessment.com/INFdysgr.htm – website containing information about dysgraphia and other disorders
www.ninds.nih.gov – National Institute Neurological Disorders and Stroke – website with information about dysgraphia and other disorders

Dyscalculia
www.dyscalculiaforum.com – website forum specifically for dyscalculia
www.dyscalculia.org – website providing information on dyscalculia
www.bdadyslexia.org.uk/dyscalculia.html – provides a short but informative review of dyscalculia

Dyspraxia
www.dyspraxiafoundation.org.uk – foundation supporting individuals and families affected by developmental dyspraxia

www.safekids.co.uk/Dyspraxia.html – information about dyspraxia
http://web.ukonline.co.uk/members/madeleine.portwood/dysprax.htm – website
about dyspraxia by Madeleine Portwood

Tourette's Syndrome
www.tourettes-action.org.uk – Tourette's Syndrome UK Association
www.tourettesyndrome.net – Tourette's Syndrome Plus website
www.lifesatwitch.com – website from Duncan McKinlay about Tourette's Syndrome
and associated disorders

Conduct Disorder
www.nice.org.uk – National Institute for Health and Clinical Excellence
www.conductdisorders.com – website providing support for parents/carers of CD

Pathological Demand Avoidance syndrome
www.pdacontact.org.uk – PDA Contact Group – website offering support to parents
of children with PDA

Starter activities
http://atschool.eduweb.co.uk/ufa10/starters/
www.quizardry.com
www.mathsisfun.net/magic.htm
www.ta-tutor.com

Brain breaks
www.brainbreaks.co.uk
www.emc.cmich.edu/BrainBreaks/
www.norfolkesinet.org.uk/pages/viewage.asp?uniqid=3458
www.braingym.org

Bibliography and further reading

Audit Commission (2002), *Special Education Needs: A Mainstream Issue*. Available at www.audit-commission.gov.uk.

Aynsley-Green, A. (2007), 'UK accused of failing children'. BBC news online (14 February 2007).

Bates, J. (1996), *Retracking* (Devon County Council).

Bavister, S. and Vickers, A. (2004), *Teach Yourself NLP* (Abingdon: Bookpoint Ltd).

Beaulieu, D. (2006), *Impact Techniques for Therapists* (Brunner-Routledge).

Beaulieu, D. (2004), *Impact Techniques in the Classroom* (Carmarthen: Crown House Publishing Ltd).

Best, B. and Thomas, W. (2007), *Everything You Need to Know About Teaching – But Are Too Busy To Ask* (London: Continuum).

Birkett, V. (2005), *How To Manage and Teach Children With Challenging Behaviour* (Cambridge: LDA).

Blakemore, S.-J. and Frith, U. (2005), *The Learning Brain – Lessons for Education* (Oxford: Blackwell Publishing).

British Medical Association (2007), 'Gambling addiction and its treatment within the NHS: A guide for health care professionals'. Available at www.bma.org.uk.

Boothman, N. (2000), *How To Make People Like You* (New York: Workman Publishing Company Inc.).

Burgess, R. (2000), *$149\frac{2}{3}$ Ways To Make Lessons Fun* (Minneapolis: Free Spirit Publishing).

Burn, G. (2005), *NLP Pocketbook* (Alresford: Management Pocketbooks Ltd).

Cavert, C. and Frank, L. and Friends (1999), *Games (and other stuff) for Teachers* (Oklahoma City: Wood and Barnes Publishing).

The Children's Society (2008), 'Good Childhood Inquiry'. Available at www.childrenssociety.org.uk.

Churches, R. and Terry, R. (2007), *NLP for Teachers* (Carmarthen: Crown House Publishing Ltd).

Ciarrochi, J. (2006), *Emotional Intelligence in Everyday Life* (Psychology Press Ltd).

Cowan, D., Palomares, S. and Schilling, D. (1994), *Skills for Teenagers* (Torrance: Inner Choice Publishing).

DCSF (2007), 'The Children's Plan' (Norwich: HMSO).

DCSF (2008), 'Personalised Learning'. Available at www.standards.dfes.gov.uk/personalisedlearning/about.

DCSF (2008), 'Personalised Learning – A Practical Guide'. Available at http://publications.teachernet.gov.uk.

De Andres, V. (1999), 'Self-esteem in the classroom or the metamorphosis of butterflies', in Arnold, J. (ed.) (1999), *Affect in Language Learning* (Cambridge: Cambridge University Press).

DfES (2007), 'Social and Emotional Aspects of Learning for Secondary Schools (SEAL), Secondary National Strategy for School Improvement'. Crown Copyright.

Dix, P. (2005), *Behaviour Management Handbook* (Lindfield: Pivotal).

Dreikurs, R., Grunwald, B. and Pepper, F. (1998), *Maintaining Sanity in the Classroom* (London: Taylor and Francis Ltd).

Dryden, G. and Vos, J. (2005), *The New Learning Revolution* (Stafford: Network Educational Press).

Dunn, R. and Dunn, K. (1998), *Learning and Teaching Styles and Brain Behaviour* (published by the Association for Supervision and Curriculum Development and the Oklahoma Department of Education Newsletter).

Faupel, A., Herrick, E. and Sharp, P. (1998), *Anger Management* (London: David Fulton Publishing).

Fisher, M. (2005), *Beating Anger* (London: Random House/Rider).

Frieman, B. (2001), *What Teachers Need to Know About Children At Risk* (New York: McGraw Hill).

Fry, W. (1970), *Sweet Madness: A Study of Humor* (Palo Alto: Pacific Books).

Funes, M. (2000), *Laughing Matters* (Dublin: Gill and Macmillan Ltd).

Gerhardt, S. (2008), 'Anger Management', *Times Educational Supplement Magazine* (17 October 2008).

Gilbert, I. (2006), *The Big Book of Independent Thinking* (Carmarthen: Crown House Publishing Ltd).

Goleman, D. (1996), *Emotional Intelligence* (London: Bloomsbury Publishing Plc).

Goleman, D. (1999), *Working With Emotional Intelligence* (London: Bloomsbury Publishing Plc).

Gradous, D. (1990), WE 59 Vol. 10 No. 5, October 1990.

Greenfield, S. (2007), *Times Educational Supplement Magazine* (12 January 2007). Source NHS Info Centre (2006).

Gregorc, A. (1982), *An Adult's Guide to Style* (Maynard, Mass.: Gabriel Systems).

HM Treasury (2003), *Every Child Matters* (The Stationery Office (TSO)). Available at www.tso.co.uk/bookshop.

Hodgson, D. (2006), *The Buzz* (Carmarthen: Crown House Publishing Ltd).

Hughes, M. and Vass, A. (2001), *Strategies for Closing the Learning Gap* (Stafford: Network).

Indiana University School of Medicine (2007), 'Research into Violent Video Games'. Available at www.research.indiana.edu.

Jackson, P. (2003), *58½ Ways To Improve Training* (Carmarthen: Crown House Publishing Ltd).

Jensen, E. (1995), *Brain Compatible Learning* (San Diego: The Brain Store).

Jensen, E. (2004), *Brain Compatible Strategies* (San Diego: The Brain Store).

Jensen, E. (2003), *Environments for Learning* (San Diego: The Brain Store).

Leaman, L. (2005), *Managing Very Challenging Behaviour* (London: Continuum).

Long, R. (2007), *The Rob Long Omnibus Edition of Better Behaviour* (Abingdon: David Fulton Publishing/Tamworth: NASEN).

Long, R. and Fogell, J. (1999), *Supporting Pupils With Emotional Difficulties* (London: David Fulton Publishers).

Mahony, T. (2007), *Making Your Words Work* (Carmarthen: Crown House Publishing Ltd).

Miller, P. (2008), *The Really Good Fun Cartoon Book of NLP* (Carmarthen: Crown House Publishing Ltd).

Moore, D. (2006), 'Education and Skills Committee – Minutes of Evidence. Oral Responses to Questions 1–47'. Available at www.publications.parliament.uk.

Morgan, P. (2008), 'Broken homes – fuel children's troubles', *Daily Mail* (22 October 2008).

Northern, S. (2004) 'Zinc and iron in diet: A rotten way to feed the children', *Times Educational Supplement* (16 April 2004).

O'Regan, F. (2005), *Surviving and Succeeding in SEN* (London: Continuum Books).

Office for National Statistics (2008), 'A Survey of the Emotional Development and Well-being of Children and Young People'. Available at www.statistics.gov.uk.

Ofsted (2008), 'Tellus 3 Survey'. Available at www.ofsted.gov.uk.

Pauc, R. (2006), *Is That My Child?* (London: Virgin Books).

Philips, M. (2008), 'Britain's criminal muddle', *Daily Mail* (26 May 2008).

Portwood, M. (1999), *Developmental Dyspraxia. Identification and Intervention Manual for Parents and Professionals* (2nd edn) (London: David Fulton Publishing).

Portwood, M. (2004), 'Something fishy's going on', *Independent* (8 July 2004).

Prashnig, B. (2006), *Learning Styles in Action* (London: Network Continuum).

The Prince's Trust (2008), 'The Culture of Youth Communities'. Available at www.princes-trust.org.uk.

Ready, R. and Burton, K. (2004), *Neuro-linguistic Programming for Dummies* (Chichester: John Wiley and Sons Ltd).

Rogers, B. (2000), *Classroom Behaviour* (London: Books Education).

SEAL, materials and guidance book available at www.teachernet.gov.uk/publication.

Smith, A. (2002), *The Brain's Behind It* (Stafford: Network).

Smith, S. (1996), *Accelerated Learning in the Classroom* (Stafford: Network).

Steer, A. (2005), 'Learning Behaviour – The report of the practitioners' group on school behaviour and discipline'. (Nottingham: DfES).

Tremblay, R., Nagin, D., S'eguin, J., Zoccolillo, M., Zelazo, P. D., Boivin, M. et al. (2004), 'Physical aggression during early childhood: Trajectories and predictors'. *Pediatrics* 114, e43–e50.

Tuckman, B. (1965), 'Developing sequence in small groups'. Available at www.in-fed.org/thinkers/tuckman.htm.

Viner, R. M. (2007), Writing for Institute of Child Health UCL.

Vizard, D. (2004), *Fuel for Thought*. Available at www.behavioursolutions.com.

Vizard. D. (2009), *Brain Breaks, Starter Activities and Fillers*. Available at www.behavioursolutions.com.

Vizard, D. (2007a), *How To Manage Behaviour In FE* (London: PCP/Sage).

Vizard, D. and Vizard, T. (2007b), *A Guide to Syndromes and Conditions*. Available at www.behavioursolutions.com.

Wallis, C. and Dell, K. (2008), 'What Makes Teens Tick?' *Time Magazine*. Available at www.time.com.

Winston. R. (2003), *The Human Mind* (London: Bantam Press).

Index